PERSPECTIVES
ON
CORPORATE
TAKEOVERS

Edited by

Thomas J. Kopp
Siena College

D1506982

UNIVERSITY
PRESS OF
AMERICA

Lanham • New York • London

Copyright © 1990 by

University Press of America,® Inc.

4720 Boston Way
Lanham, MD 20706

3 Henrietta Street
London WC2E 8LU England

Printed in the United States of America

British Cataloging in Publication Information Available

Library of Congress Cataloging-in-Publication Data

Perspectives on corporate takeovers / edited by Thomas J. Kopp.
        p.   cm.
Papers from a symposium held at Siena College, Loudonville, N.Y.
Bibliography: p.
Includes index.
1. Consolidation and merger of corporations—Congresses.   I. Kopp, Thomas J.
    HD2746.5.P47   1989   338.8'3—dc20   89–34286 CIP

ISBN 0–8191–7515–3 (alk. paper)
ISBN 0–8191–7516–1 (pbk.: alk. paper)

All University Press of America books are produced on acid-free paper.
The paper used in this publication meets the minimum requirements of American
National Standard for Information Sciences—Permanence of Paper for Printed Library
Materials, ANSI Z39.48–1984.   ∞

This volume is dedicated to those at Siena College who supported and organized the conference upon which this work is based, especially Siena's President, Father Hugh F. Hines, O.F.M., and Dean of Business Dr. Douglas A. Lonnstrom; and my special thanks to my wife Gail, who helped type the manuscript and tolerated the hours I committed to it.

Contents

Introduction

The articles presented in <u>Perspectives on Corporate Takeovers</u> originated as papers and addresses presented at Siena College in Loudonville, New York. That symposium, "Mergers and Acquisitions: the Hundredth Year" recognized the one hundredth year of Federal involvement in the regulation of business, which began with the Interstate Commerce Commission in 1887. Like the ICC, which began by focusing its energies on such great trust builders as Carnegie, Morgan, and Rockefeller, our conference sought to focus upon a wave of restructuring. This second great wave that has descended upon us takes the form of mergers, acquisitions, buy-backs and leveraged buy-outs.

At Siena College we believe that the conference achieved our objectives. As a Liberal Arts College with a strong Franciscan tradition, we wanted to bring together a diverse group of practitioners and academics to facilitate the opening of a meaningful and stimulating dialogue. We believe that this book furthers that goal. Through pooling the experiences of those who have participated in Mergers and Acquisitions with the research of academics, this book offers the reader a unique opportunity to assess the merger wave engulfing our economy.

The articles presented embody the experiences and concerns of conference participants. Those written by CEO's - Victor Riley of Key-corp, an acquirer, and J. Patrick Barrett of AVIS, who was acquired several times - both focus upon the concerns of overall viability. The details of making such a merger a success at SMC Corporation are explored by Raymond Thoren, whereas Lawrence Huggins chronicles a failure. An empirical view concerning whether such combinations can achieve sustainable growth is explored by John Clark, Margaret Clark, and Gerard Olson. John Funicello of the AFL-CIO presents the merger and acquisition issue from the perspective of the worker. The impact on shareholders is explored empirically by Antony Cherin and Michael Hergert, whereas Mark Gardner examines the impact of a raid by Mesa Partners. The implications of this activity for the entire economy are explored by Thomas Kopp and Paul Ruggeri in an examination of Research and Development spending, whereas John Clark, Thomas Chiang, Alok Chakrabarti and Gerard Olson examine the causal factors of this national event. In addition, Douglas Mayer presents a lively contrast by seeking insight into Mergers and

Acquisitions from medieval literature, whereas Michael Murphy examines a merger of educational institutions.

Each of these articles provides insight into different perspectives on how the impact of acquisitions should be assessed. They illustrate a diverse range of concerns as well as issues which all principled individuals must grapple with.

Our hope is that this book furthers your understanding of each perspective, and contributes to the formulation of a consensus public policy which is both economically efficient and ethical.

Thomas J. Kopp
Department of Finance
Siena College

PERSPECTIVE OF AN ACQUISITIONS VETERAN[1]

by

J. Patrick Barrett[2]

I am very pleased to participate in this extremely important symposium. As you know, I am a graduate of Siena College and that makes me especially proud, and honored, to be here today. I came here a young man who wanted to learn, and who also wanted to play basketball, and I left here a businessman. My education has certainly stood me in good stead throughout the years since I walked this campus every day.

Given today's virtual frenzy of merger and acquisition activity, I think a symposium of this kind is vital. The fact is, America needs to communicate on this topic. All of us (representatives from various industries, labor, academia, government, finance) need to share our experiences and perspectives. I think that today's symposium will go far toward advancing an understanding of each other's perspectives, and I salute the fine work of Siena College in developing this program.

First, I'd like to give you some background. In the past four years, Avis has experienced four acquisitions ...which is why I've title my address the "Perspective of an Acquisitions Veteran". During those years, I have seen positive things happen to my company and I have, in all honesty, seen negative effects as well. Obviously, as the chairman and chief executive officer, it is my charter to make Avis a healthy, profitable organization, pleasing investors and customers, providing stable employment opportunities, and building and safeguarding our company's future. I'm sure you can appreciate that this has not been the easiest of tasks, in light of the frequent change of ownership.

I'd also like to point out that I am an investor. Like all investors, I am concerned about realizing healthy returns on my investments. I know first-hand

---

[1] This was a keynote address given at Siena College's Symposium on Mergers and Acquisitions

[2] Chairman of Carpat Investments, Ltd and former Chairman & Chief Executive Officer of Avis, Inc.

the effects that mergers and acquisitions can have on them.

Now, about Avis. The company has a history of changing owners that spans the four decades since its inception. Over those years, Avis has experienced 11 different periods of ownership. Avis started with the vision of a young World War II army officer, back in 1946. Warren Avis foresaw the rapid development of commercial aviation in the post war era, and established the first Avis Rent A Car location at Willow Run Airport in Detroit. He is credited with being the first to set up a rent a car operations at airports.

In 1954, Avis sold the company to a Boston investor and car rental operator, Richard S. Robie, who in turn sold Avis to a group of Boston investors, headed by William Tetrick, in 1956. The growing organization was then purchased by the international banking firm, Lazard Freres and Co., in 1962. Less than a year later, Avis introduced the "we try harder" campaign, which was to become one of the most effective advertising slogans in history, and helped make Avis a household name.

As a household name in American business, with a worldwide network and a sound profit picture, Avis was selected for acquisition in 1965 by ITT Corporation, at the time the most successful corporate conglomerate in American history. In 1973, ITT came under a federal court order to divest itself of certain properties, including Avis. Avis then operated as a publicly-owned company listed on the New York Stock Exchange, under the guidance of a court-appointed trustee, until it was acquired by Norton Simon, in 1977.

Then, in 1983, Esmark purchased Norton Simon, including Avis. In 1984, Beatrice Co. purchased Esmark, including Avis, and in 1985, Avis was part of the $6.2 billion leveraged buyout of Beatrice companies by Kohlberg, Kravis, Roberts and Co. That purchase was made, however, with the intention of divesting Avis. And, in July of 1986, Avis was purchased by its management and Wesray Capital Corporation, through a leveraged buyout. At age forty, Avis acquired yet another, and its current, parent. We've survived and we are prospering!

And our experience has given us as a company, and has given me personally, a range of first-hand information about many of the effects and aspects of acquisitions. In fact, at Avis we sometimes feel that we're not only experts at renting cars, but also at being owned by others. Notably, the purchase by the management and Wesray marked the first time in nine years that Avis had been sold as a single entity. In other words, by a group that sought to buy the company. And we believe that we will now find the stability that we have needed.

Wesray, as you may know, is owned by William E. Simon, former Secretary of the United States Treasury, and his partner Raymond Chambers. Wesray looks at a potential acquisition in terms of solid, capable management, a good profit record, and outstanding growth possibilities, and Avis is pleased to be put in that category. Avis today employs 21,000 people worldwide, and has a fleet of approximately 300,000 vehicles. And we certainly believe we will realize our growth potential. Avis is, in fact, growing faster than the rent a car industry as a whole, and in 1986, the industry showed about a ten percent gain in revenue over the previous year. In December, we announced the start of a new franchise operation, Avis Lube, which will provide consumers with quick and convenient lubrication of their cars, and with associated services.

I joined Avis as chairman and chief executive officer in 1981, having been the chief financial officer at Norton Simon. I basically consider myself capable of adapting to various styles of management, but that ability has been put to the test several times through these past years. I'm sure you can appreciate that, when the industry as a whole faced serious problems due to rising costs, we at Avis experienced a tightening of control from our parent companies. Now, however, it is Wesray's policy to leave the management of its acquisitions intact, and to practice a hands-off ownership style.

The contrast in styles between various parents points to the many contrasts and contrasting viewpoints encompassed in the merger and acquisitions issue. For example, on the one extreme, there is the position that takeovers are generally a boon to American business, because they consistently benefit shareholders, replace management that is inefficient, and result in better use of assets. Obviously, this carries with it a desire for placing severe limitations on defensive actions.

On the other side of the spectrum there is the position that takeovers consistently deplete companies that are healthy, that they focus management attention primarily on the short-term, that they result in dangerously high debt levels, and have a severe impact on employees and communities. And, obviously, with this viewpoint comes the call for strict controls on takeovers. There is sufficient room between these two perspectives to accommodate each of us here today .

Personally and professionally, while I believe there is merit to both positions, I am very much in favor of acquisitions, when planned and implemented carefully and reasonably. Let me explain. It is essential to note that mergers and acquisitions are very much about growth. A key element in the overall strategy of any business is, of course, how to grow; whether to develop new products, markets, or to otherwise expand. And, recently, external growth opportunities have become extremely attractive.

Mergers and acquisitions are not necessarily ends in themselves, but means; the means to grow in an era of unprecedented competition. Please note that I'm not talking solely about profit. I'm talking about a corporation realizing its potential (consistently attaining its maximum market value) both today and tomorrow. To chart a path of true growth, a corporation must consider all of the elements that are involved in, or impacted by, both its short-term and long-term performance. Consideration must be given to the owners (whether private or public), the board of directors, the management, the customers, the employees, the community, and all other corporate entities.

Obviously, achieving the balance of all of these considerations is not easily accomplished. But this balance is what business must strive for, regardless of who is running the corporation. Stockholders and managers alike must make this their goal. The corporation is a complex, living organization that goes through phases and changes, just as the people who comprise it do. Certainly, we are in a major phase right now.

In the 60s and 70s, we saw an emphasis on corporate diversification, which we now see reversing. We are seeing corporations divest themselves of many holdings that do not fit closely with their primary business. We have seen major deregulation in a number of industries and now see companies of like pursuits link together to strengthen operations and achieve efficiencies of scale. We are seeing a group of entrepreneurs step in and claim that they can manage

4

our corporations better. We are seeing creative financing techniques support these activities. And we are seeing all this in the face of competition that gives American companies grave worries not only about growth, but also about survival. And we need to be efficient to survive. If an acquisition (or the potential of an acquisition) results in redirecting our focus and resources, and results in greater efficiency, with an eye toward both short-term profitability and long-term growth, it can be a very positive thing. It is my hope that, ultimately, this period in American corporate history will result in all of us finding our way back to achieving the path to true growth.

Another issue that has surfaced from all of this merger and acquisition activity is the new emphasis on stockholders' rights. In a corporation the stockholders, the board of directors and management all play critical roles in charting the company's success and future. We cannot lose sight of the fact that, in such a structure, the stockholders are those at risk. And they have the right of ultimate control. I am not an advocate of takeovers for takeovers' sake, or for the quick profit stockholders can gain as a result of ravaging a company. We all know the difference between growth and greed. However, on the other hand, I do think that in many instances, a merger or acquisition can breathe new life into a company, and can help strong businesses become even stronger.

Avis, I think, provides an excellent example of a company that can be strengthened by its recent acquisition. It is essential, however, that any such merger or acquisition (or any defensive move) be taken with a view of the future as well as the present. For instance, short-term profits should not and do not have to mean that long-term investments (in R & D, for one) must suffer, and research bears this point out. On the other hand, long-term planning does not necessarily mean that today's stock prices must be depressed. I call for managers and shareholders alike to keep both short and long term goals in sight.

Clearly, mergers and acquisitions bring with them a host of serious questions, particularly about personnel. Employee morale and layoffs, and the far reaching, attendant economic ramifications, are of course, key concerns. However, those are not linked to mergers and acquisitions only. The duplication of departments is a personnel issue directly linked to mergers and acquisitions, as is the fate of management. I believe that we must make a sincere effort to consider all of our employees' well-being to the greatest extent possible. We should certainly try to accommodate personnel whose departments will be cut.

Given the frequent changes that occur as Avis moves from one owner to another, we are frequently asked about the morale of our employees. Frankly, many employees have not experienced a direct impact. But those who have, have handled the situation admirably. The Avis group is a resilient, committed lot -- with a genuine desire to get the job done well, regardless of who our ultimate parent is. We are extremely proud of our people, because they are why the "we try harder" spirit is very much alive and well at Avis today. And management makes a continuous effort to communicate with our employees, apprise them of developments, and keep morale high. And, of course, we are careful to minimize layoffs. However, when we found it imperative to make a significant labor cut a few years ago, we did our best to assist those employees with severance pay, and extended benefits for those who had not found new positions by a certain time.

On the issue of management, I believe that the arrival of new owners does not necessarily signal the devastation of a company's management team -- and I am a living example. I want to point out that I do not perceive acquisitions as across-the-board signals of bad management -- and research, as well as my own experience, supports that statement. On the other hand, change in management is sometimes imperative (and not linked only to mergers and acquisitions). Such issues do highlight the need for planning and managing a merger or acquisition as much as planning and managing a corporation. It is a dynamic process, with a myriad of considerations, that requires skilled, experienced implementers and overseers.

At the outset, companies need to carefully compare their strategies as well as their organizations, to achieve as smooth a transition, and as fine a fit, as possible. Mergers and acquisitions should not be questions of simply working to make deals, but of working to make those deals work. Reports indicate that 1986 saw more than $150 billion worth of merger and acquisition activity, wherein the transaction figures were disclosed. We've seen mergers and acquisitions spread across American industry...notably in retailing, airline and communications, and in the rent a car business, too. Over the past one and one-half years, all of the four major rent a car companies (Avis, Hertz, National and Budget) have changed ownership. It is projected that this level of activity will go even higher in 1987, what with continued low interest rates, available money and foreign investments. That raises serious questions for the future.

We all wonder about the ability of companies that have incurred so much debt to withstand an economic downturn or a recession, and that is why I urge the path of reason. I believe that risk can make business great -- but so, too, can a rational approach to that risk. It is essential to balance the two. That, I believe, is the challenge we now face, whether managers or investors. Growth can be exhilarating. But we all know that it can also exact a measure of discomfort or pain. In analyzing today's merger and acquisition activity, we need to be mindful of the expense associated with preparing to grow and profit in today's global economy, and we also need to be mindful of the expense of not preparing to grow and profit.

A COMMON SENSE APPROACH TO MERGERS AND ACQUISITIONS[1]

by

Victor J. Riley[2]

You're all nearing the end of a full and interesting day. But, I hope you have enough stamina left to hear one more perspective on a subject that's caused more commotion in the business community than almost anything else in recent years. Of course, I'm talking about corporate mergers and acquisitions.... or merger mania as it's been labelled.

Merger mania has swept into America's public consciousness. It's now big-time news and Madison Avenue fodder. For instance, one night a few weeks ago, I was watching the late show on t.v.. It was one of those Japanese science fiction movies. The kind where Godzilla defends the earth against some hideous monster that's trying to destroy civilization...sort of like the S.E.C. going after Ivan Boesky.

While I was watching the movie, an interesting commercial came on. It was for Bulova watches. The ad depicted a merger deal in the making. Two groups of yuppies glared at each other from opposite sides of a conference table. They struggled throughout the night to reach an agreement....filling the room with frowns and violent gestures. A happy ending seemed hopeless. But when morning finally came, the deal was somehow done. Smiles replaced frowns. Everyone was happy. Then, to end this little saga, a narrator announced that a designer watch would be a perfect gift to reward these valiant corporate heroes. Now, you know that something's a hot topic when it's glamorized to sell status symbols to Mr. and Mrs. Jones watching the late show. M and A's are indeed a hot topic. And for good reason.

The merger and acquisition activity of recent years is unprecedented in scope. There was a record high of $144 billion in disclosed M and A volume in 1985. And last year's total exceeded that with a total of $158 billion. It's really a mega-billion dollar whirlwind. As evidenced by stories on deals and rumors

---

[1] This was a keynote address given at Siena College's Symposium on Mergers and Acquisitions

[2] President and Chief Executive Officer of KeyCorp

of deals appearing almost every day in the Wall Street Journal.

My company has been involved in a few such stories. As chief executive officer of Keycorp, I head a firm that has been very active on the acquisition front. Actually, that's an understatement. Keycorp is one of America's fastest-growing financial institutions....due, in large part, to our aggressive interstate acquisitions program. So, I'm a front-line participant in the M and A game. And I have some practical views to share with you, based on my experiences and observations.

The message that I want to leave with you tonight is this: corporate America needs to adopt a sensible approach to mergers and acquisitions.

Surely, M and A's are a beneficial and necessary component of our economic system. But some of what has become rather common means of implementing them, or thwarting them, can seriously damage otherwise viable business. Junk-bond buyouts, poison pills, and greenmail have all come into vogue. Measures like these can often bring about more regress than progress for the companies involved. And, that's the exact opposite of what carefully and responsibly conceived M and A deals should accomplish.

American business needs to reemphasize cooperative agreements for business consolidations...and to pursue M and A ventures that make for more efficient allocation and use of capital...instead of excursions that foolishly drain resources.

This point seems clear in view of our current business environment. But let me back up for a moment. Sometimes, it's good to look at the past to gain perspective on the present. Let's go back to the turn of the century... The late 1890's to 1900...when America had its first great wave of merger and acquisition activity.

This was an era of drastic change in America's business landscape. Barons of industry like Andrew Carnegie, George Pullman and H. C. Frick bought out competitors and service enterprises at will to expand their powerful trusts. These trusts, in industries such as iron, steel, coal, copper, tobacco, and railroads, came to dominate American business...growing through both friendly and coercive consolidations.

For example, from 1898 to 1900 there were 50 mergers and acquisitions in the steel and iron industries alone. The Sherman Anti-Trust Act was largely ignored, and would remain so for another decade. This was the birth of big business...as America achieved the promise of industrialization and a continent-wide economic system. Our nation was embarking on the greatest period of speculation and business advance that had ever taken place up to that time.

Today, almost a century later, American business is undergoing it's greatest restructuring since the days of the great robber barons...the restructuring of the late 1980's. In recent years, we've witnessed a frenzy of mergers, acquisitions, buybacks, spinoffs, leveraged buy-outs and recapitalizations. American business hasn't seen this much action since 1901, when J. P. Morgan merged three industrial trusts into the world's first $1 billion corporation.

It's been estimated that some 4,000 of today's largest companies spent nearly $200 billion to transform themselves last year...streamlining their operations or taking on synergistic business to strengthen market positions. Mergers and acquisitions have played an important role in this movement---which has made many companies more efficient. Certainly, we all agree that well-conceived mergers and acquisitions are an engine of progress for corporate America. But, I'm here to talk about the dark side of this story.

It's a fact that the business world has always had a certain number of stupid people doing stupid things. America has experienced several great waves of M and A activity, and they've all had their share of inane deals. Much of the trouble, as I mentioned earlier, stems from junk bond takeovers and related poison pill defenses---new twists that have exploded onto the M and A scene in the past few years.

Right now, in this age of junk bond deals, virtually no public company is immune from a takeover threat. Even the largest companies are targets. And these days, the small can devour the big. Lone corporate raiders and overzealous companies are snaring firms whose resources greatly exceed their own. Some folks on wall street love this...the market's climbed and fortunes have been made packaging deals. Some dreamers and schemers in corporate America love it too. It's their weapon to hunt big game for big profits. But many may just wind up shooting themselves in the foot, or even more vital parts of their corporate anatomy.

Mountains of debt have been amassed by some speculators using junk bonds to reach beyond their means. Right now, about $20 billion in debt is outstanding in junk bond takeovers. Too many buyers in such leveraged takeovers seem to be overestimating themselves...gaining control of comparatively larger organizations which they may not have the capacity to manage.

And what of the post-merger corporation saddled with excessive debt? Future profits could be eroded for years to come. Funds for research, capital improvements, and personnel will be cut. Management will inevitably shift its focus from long-term growth to short-term survival...all to the detriment of progress.

Worse yet, excessive debt can become a crippling burden for such companies in an economic downturn. Like walking a tightrope on a blustery day, there would be precious little room for error. The more highly leveraged takeovers we see now, the more business failures we may see when the economy eventually goes soft.

Obviously, Paul Volcker spotted those dangers himself. That's why the Fed placed its 50% cap on junk bond takeover financing last year. This will help to curb excesses, but it won't halt them. Now I'm sure you all know that the number of junk bond takeovers is declining. The main reason for this is simple. In M and A warfare, the defense is catching up with the offense. A growing number of managements confronted with takeover threats are using poison pills to ward off potential raiders.

This is nothing to cheer about. It's not a case of good guys versus bad guys...besieged managements versus evil raiders. Poison pill defenses are getting more and more extreme. They're terribly destructive forces if used recklessly. They can tear a company apart more explosively than a bust-up takeover. Some are so insidious, they're even making a sympathetic figure out of T. Boone Pickens---and that's pretty hard to do. Mr. Pickens' new lobbying group, the United Shareholders Association of America, is great P.R. vehicle, but it's also been ironically on-target in publicizing the dangers of poison pill abuses.

Meanwhile, in this battleground of junk bond takeovers and poison pills, another dangerous abuse is spreading---greenmail. Here, the hostile takeover threat is just a shadow dance to extort cash. Sometimes though, it's hard to tell who the culprits really are in a greenmail drama. Is it a greedy speculator who's after easy money? Or is it a bloated management determined to stay entrenched at any cost? Either way, it's the company's loyal shareholders---the real owners---who'll have to pay in the long run.

Likewise, whether it's an irresponsible junk bond takeover...or a reckless resort to poison pills...or the near-larceny of greenmail...the end result is the same, wasted energy, wasted resources, regress in corporate America. Still, I would be very reluctant to call for further anti-takeover legislation at this point. Senator Proxmire's Democratic-controlled banking committee will probably push for some in 1987. But, it's very dangerous to shackle the free marketplace any more than absolutely necessary.

Instead, the business community should look to itself for the solutions to its M and A problems. Business leaders must call for...and carry out...more responsibility in mergers and acquisitions. The task is part education and part teaching by example, with both going hand-in-hand. Then, perhaps we can make strides toward achieving a more common sense approach to merger mania.

Let me give you an example...one that typifies the kind of common sense approach I'm calling for. It's a quick case study from Keycorp's own experience. The subject: our acquisition of the $100 million Bank of Oregon in 1985.

Two years ago, the Bank of Oregon was in deep trouble. It was a rapidly failing institution. Assets were dropping, lending was at a standstill, the federal government had to step in with aid. When the F.D.I.C. sought out potential buyers to save the bank, Keycorp responded. Why?

Well, for some time, our management had been planning to expand Keycorp's banking network into the Pacific northwest---a region that we think holds great promise for economic growth as America's trade window to the far east. Today, this bank---now Key Bank of Oregon---is performing beyond anyone's expectations. It's a healthy and growing institution...it's adding to Keycorp's bottom line...and it's helping to fuel the local economy.

13

Now, consider the critical elements of this brief case-in-point. This acquisition was made foresight...cooperation...and responsible financial orchestration. It has resulted in benefits for all sides.

That's typical of Keycorp's approach to M and A's. Our company is both a proponent and practitioner of responsible M and A activity. Over the years, Keycorp has made more than 25 acquisitions, and they've all been friendly marriages, which is notable in today's world of hostile takeovers. We believe that cooperation is a key to real success in acquisitions.

Sure, hostile takeovers have a valid place in business as a means to dislodge chronically inefficient management. But, if you're going to deplete a company's resources and alienate its employees in a takeover fight, then it just might not be a battle worth winning. Courtships are less expensive, sometimes a bit more time-consuming, but certainly more productive than hostile takeovers. They also lay the groundwork for assimilating new employees and operations more efficiently. And, the friendlier you are with a target company before final discussions, the more you'll be able to discover about its inner workings before a deal is struck.

Here are seven basic guidelines that I would present to companies for sensible M and A behavior:

First and foremost, never take on excessive debt to finance an acquisition. You can't build for the future by mortgaging it away.

Second...balance the methods of financing used in M and A's. This is especially important for companies, like Keycorp, that have a vigorous acquisition program. Total abstinence from debt, on the other hand, is just as stupid as complete reliance on it. We try to balance our equity financing with judicious use of debt.

Third...avoid serious earnings dilution at all costs. Prolonged dilution either means you've made a dumb acquisition, you're not managing it effectively, or you paid too much in the first place. We have a guideline for this. Keycorp will not make any acquisition that we think could materially dilute earnings for more than 12 to 18 months.

Fourth...simply stated, always seek value. Be sure that the acquisition you make will add to your company's bottom line---in the short-run. And refuse to pay an inflated price tag. Keycorp has not paid more than 1.7 times book value for any acquisition candidate so far. We think that's a reasonable ceiling given our markets and our industry---and we'll continue to try and operate within this parameter.

Fifth, get to know the people who make up the target company. Meet the rank-&-file employees before a deal is signed. Assess their needs and concerns. Analyze their corporate culture and make sure it would mesh with your own. Everything in the human equation must be compatible.

Sixth...Before the acquisition is finalized, know every detail about the target company's operations. This sounds elementary, but you might be surprised at how blind some corporate acquisitions are. As I mentioned in the Bank of Oregon example, Keycorp worked hard to identify every weakness...identify every strength...and determine exactly how to manage an acquisition candidate for maximum performance---prior to signing the agreement.

And finally...here's one more seemingly obvious rule that too many businesses violate: only make acquisitions that fit in with your company's long-term strategy. For an acquisition to be at all worthwhile, it has to help achieve some of your company's most important future goals and priorities.

Now to sum up, a consistent philosophy combining all these elements is the basis for an intelligent and responsible approach to M and A's. We think that we've achieved this at Keycorp. And, I hope that our experience can serve as a model for other companies embarking on M and A activity.

Corporate America will always need the positive restructuring effect of mergers and acquisitions...which pump fresh blood and build stronger muscle in our economy. But the dangers in today's reckless M and A sub-world of junk bonds and poison pills are very real. So, once again, I'll state my refrain: The business community needs to develop a more common sense approach to mergers and acquisitions.

Too bad common sense isn't like the common cold...something you can't avoid catching. The trouble is, it can be quite elusive. That's why business leaders and academic leaders who recognize the problems discussed here should speak out to educate corporate America. If we can teach business to act more responsibly in its continuous hop-scotch of M and A dealmaking, then companies will benefit...shareholders will benefit...employees will benefit...and customers will benefit. In short, America's entire economy will benefit, and that's a noble goal for us to reach for in the year ahead.

THE IMPACT OF ACQUISITIONS ON THE
SCM CORPORATION - 1966-1986

OR

THE SHORT HAPPY LIFE OF A
CORPORATE CONGLOMERATE

by

Professor Raymond Thoren [1]

Introduction

The selection of the SCM Corporation and its
acquisition activities is particularly appropriate as
this Symposium is taking place in Upstate New York and
the SCM Corporation, the old Smith Corona Marchant
Corporation, was originally located in syracuse and for
many years had a typewriter manufacturing plant in
Cortland.

My involvement with SCM ran from February 1966 to
1978. From 1966 to 1970 I worked in the corporate
development department and was actively involved in all
of the conglomerate acquisitions that took place during
that time. From 1970 to 1978, I was controller of one
of the companies that we had acquired.

Examining the activities of SCM from 1966 to 1986
should be of particular interest to this group because
it involves analyzing the motivating factors for the
conglomerate wave of the 1960's and the takeover wave
of the 1980's. During the conglomerate wave it was SCM
doing the acquiring but in January 1986, it was Hanson
Trust PLC, a British Company, taking over SCM. Hanson
immediately proceeded to sell off the conglomerate
acquisitions and undo what SCM had put together over
that 20 year period.

The SCM Corporation in 1966

SCM, in 1966, was a business equipment company
with sales of $220 million and the following product
lines:
                Portable Typewriters
                Office Typewriters

---

[1] Currently Area Coordinator, Accounting and
Finance, SUNY at Plattsburgh and a former manger in the
Acquisition and Mergers Department of SCM Corp.

        Calculators (Marchant)
        Adding Machines
        Data Processing
        Bookkeeping Equipment
        Teletype Equipment (Kleinschmidt)
        Photocopiers (using coated paper)

All of the above product lines would disappear during the period from 1966 to 1986 except for the portable typewriter and teletype division.

The Marchant Calculator and the SCM Adding Machine, would go out of existence because of SCM's inability to adapt to the dramatic change which saw the old electro-mechanical calculator replaced by the electronic calculator. The technologically oriented companies such as Hewlett-Packard, Texas Instruments and the Japanese manufacturers became the dominant factors in a business they had not previously been in at all.

The Data Processing Equipment which manufactured bookkeeping machines to perform payroll and billing work never made any money and was eventually sold to Control Data. Office typewriters eventually met the same fate as SCM was never able to make any inroads into IBM's 75% market share.

The photocopy business was the rapid growth business of the 1960's and the main reason for the rise in sales, E.P.S. and the P/E ratio. The SCM copier was one that required coated paper. It competed with Xerox on a price basis and had no long term viability. A major research report was published by Equity Research Associates in 1967 called "Xerox and the Seven Dwarfs." The dwarfs, like SCM are mostly extinct today.

SCM attempted to enter the plain paper copier business with a joint venture arrangement but this was also unsuccessful. The final failure was a $1.3 billion anti-trust law suit against Xerox that lasted one year and had minimal success.

As stated before, most the product line in existence in 1966 were not around in 1986. This is significant because the companies that were taken over, were taken over by a company, who, for the most part, had no future without them.

18

Motivation for SCM's Conglomerate Activities

The two previous periods of high merger activity 1896 to 1905 and 1920 to 1929. Both of these periods were characterized by a rising stock market. The conglomerate wave of the 1960's was no different. The Dow Jones Industrial Average hit an all time high of 1000 during the first quarter of 1966. The rising market value of a company's common stock was a major impetus to acquire other companies because the rising market value also meant an increase in the Price-Earnings Ratio. SCM saw its price-earnings ratio rise to between 22-30 times earnings during this period. The rise in a company's P/E ratio meant that you could acquire companies with lower P/E ratios and have an instant increase in your earnings per share. In the 1960's, in many cases, there was also an instant increase in the market value of the common stock.

SCM's higher price earnings rise was primarily the result of two factors.
1. The rising stock market. (DJI hit 1000 during this period.)
2. An accelerating growth in sales and earnings which resulted primarily from the rise in photocopy sales and earnings.

Ironically, both of these were short lived factors because the Dow Jones Industrial Average would not touch 1000 again until the 1980's and SCM's photocopy business would disappear completely over the next ten years.

SCM's Acquisitions

The major conglomerate acquisitions and dates were as follows:

Dates	Company	Product Line
Mar. 1966	Proctor Silex	Appliances-Irons-Toasters
Sept. 1966	Shetland Lewyt	Appliances-Vacuum Cleaners
May 1967	Glidden Corp.	Paint-Foods-Chemicals
Sept. 1967	Allied Paper	Pulp and Paper
Sept. 1968	Melabs	High-Tech Equipment

Proctor Silex was the first significant acquisition during the 1960's and was made at a time when the Dow

Jones Industrial Average was approaching 1000. The acquisition added $.30 to SCM's E.P.S. and the price of SCM's stock doubled over the next six weeks form $46 to $92. Proctor Silex stock rose from $10 that Proctor Silex was selling at on the American Exchange. While appliances were not related to business equipment the combination was viewed favorably by the stock market. Proctor Silex over the 20 year period was a marginal contributor to SCM's earnings and was sold to William Simon, former Secretary of the Treasury and prominent investment banker in 1983. Simon purchased the company using leveraged buyout techniques and along with his other purchases which included Anchor Hocking Glass and Wearever Corporation reaped huge personal benefits. SCM recorded a $6 million loss because the sale was made at less than book value.

Shetland-Lewyt was an appliance company manufacturing primarily vacuum cleaners with sales of $20 mm and substantial year to year losses. The acquisition had no impact on the market value of the stock. It was made because the belief was that successful appliance management of Proctor Silex would be able to take this company and turn it around. Vast efforts were made but no success was achieved. What was found out was that vacuum cleaners were considerably different from other appliances and Shetlands acceptance in the market place was week. The acquisition was a total mistake. The business was shut down and the assets were sold.

Glidden Corporation was the most significant acquisition in SCM's Corporate history. It was larger than SCM at the time of acquisition (approximately $260 million sales versus $240 million) and was available because of a take-over attempt by the Great American Corporation, a Texas Insurance Company. SCM was one of 30 white knights who rushed to the rescue and the deal was made over the weekend following the Friday take over announcement in the Wall Street Journal. Great America's offer was $30 or a $9 premium over the $21 market value of Glidden. SCM upped the offer to $35. SCM's market value at the date of the announcement was $79 and in spite of the fact that Glidden added $.35 to SCM's E.P.S., SCM's market value began to decline.

Glidden was a solid company with a Durkee Food and Glidden Paint Division plus a chemical division that was to become the "Crown Jewel" of the entire SCM Corporate. The real mystery here was why Glidden, from among the many suitors, chose SCM. SCM's product lines and future growth was far more inferior than the solid base bread and butter businesses that Glidden had developed. The only explanation was that SCM's participation in the photocopy industry and Glidden managements perception of the future prospects of this industry caused them to select SCM. THis perception proved to be an incorrect one and Glidden Shareholders watched SCM's market value drop from $79 to $9. They also saw SCM commit substantial funds to the photocopy industry and to a major anti-trust law suit against Xerox that lasted one year and gained nothing. Glidden shareholders would never see $79 again and would receive a fraction of their purchasing power when SCM was taken over at $75 a share in 1986.

Allied Paper proved to be the second most significant acquisition in spite of the fact that at the time it was an undercapitalized paper company primarily utilizing the de-inking process and having obsolete plants that had been constructed in the 19th century. Allied was acquired because it had the Allied-Egry business forms division, a business that SCM was interested in a getting involved. Allied was acquired in September 1967. By this time, SCM's stock had dropped to $47 a share and Allied's acquisition, which made no significant contribution to SCM's E.P.S., did nothing to stop the decline.

Melabs was a high technology company with declining sales and earnings and was purchased because the company had research oriented, high technology personnel and because it was believed that the company was a turnaround situation. The lack of high technology personnel was a major consideration for SCM at that time because the advent of chip technology was causing a major technological change in the calculator industry. SCM, because of its inability to adapt to the changing technology, eventually shut down its Marchant Calculator Division and the calculator industry soon became dominated by companies like Texas Instrument and Hewlett-Packard not to mention the Japanese companies. Melabs was the second acquisition disaster. Its instrument division was sold but the rest of the business was written off.

Other acquisitions, including the Histacount Corporation, Walton Business Forms, the titanium dioxide acquisition in the 1980's are not commented on here because they were either minor acquisitions of a favorable nature or were expansions of existing product lines.

Some Comments on the Conglomerate Period

Unlike the first two merger waves, which are from 1895 to 1906 and 1920 to 1929, which were primarily balance sheet driven or asset oriented, the conglomerate wave of the 1960's, was income statement and earnings per share oriented. The criteria we used to determine suitable acquisition candidate at SCM was simple. We looked for company's with P/E ratios that were lower than ours. When we found one we went through numerous financial calculations to determine how much of a premium we could offer and still make a contribution to our earnings per share.

Accounting principles in the 1960's as they related to pooling of interests versus purchase accounting and to the computations of earnings per share were weak. The conglomerate period has sometimes been characterized as a period when acquisition minded companies took advantage of weakly structured accounting principles as they related to pooling and earnings per share computations. For SCM, the ideal mechanics for an acquisition was pooling of interest accounting, no E.P.S. dilution from contingent securities and a tax-free reorganization decision by the IRS on behalf of the seller. All of these in the 1960's were easily attainable. The abuses of this period caused the accounting profession to release Accounting Principle Bulletins Number 15 which required all potentially dilutive securities such as warrants, options convertibles and contingent securities to be reflected in a "fully diluted" earnings per share computation.

The early 1970's saw a dramatic decline in the market value of conglomerate stocks and thus the beginning of a long period of low plea's for conglomerates. SCM's market value dropped to $9 and remained in the high teens for the next nine years. Litton Industries, Gulf and Western and the other major conglomerates fared no better.

Takeover of SCM by Hanson Trust Plc. - September 1985

Hanson Trust first offered $60 a share at a time when the SCM market value was $48. The eventual takeover price would be $75 which still proved to be a bargain for Hanson. SCM management fought fiercely to avoid the takeover by enlisting the Merrill Lynch Capital Group and worked out a deal where the "Crown Jewels" the two most profitable segments of the corporation, sold to the Merrill Lynch group at a

22

stipulated price if the takeover proceeded. SCM lost
their case in the courts and in January 1986. were
taken over. By August 1986, the major pulp and paper
operations of Allied and the Glidden Paint Division had
already been sold and Hanson was well on its way to
reaping a huge profit from the transaction.

Why SCM Was a Vulnerable Take-Over Target

Over the 20 year period 1966-86, SCM's sales grew
from $220 million to $2.2 billion approximately 10
times while net income and earnings per share also saw
substantial increases. If you could take SCM's P/E
ratio of the 1960's and multiply it times the E.P.S. of
the 1980's, the stock's market value before the
takeover, instead of being $48, would have been in the
$120-$160 range. THis means that all of the
substantial progress by SCM in increasing sales and
earnings was never recognized by the financial
community and never reflected in the market value of
the stock. It thus clearly had reached a point where
the sum of the parts was worth substantially more than
the whole. SCM management was perhaps on the verge of
recognizing this fact as witnessed by the sale of the
Proctor-Silex Division to William Simon, although Simon
managed to negotiate the sale at a $6 mm loss to SCM.

Two takeover attempts in 1980 and 1981 plus the
increased activity in the areas of takeovers and
leveraged buy-outs should have alerted the SCM
management to their potential vulnerability. SCM
management never owned many shares in the company
(probably though the market price would never rise).
Poison pills or other defensive measures could have
been taken but weren't. SCM management had fought off
three major take-over attempts in 1957 (Rapid-American
Corp), 1980(Petrocelli Clothes Co.) and 1981(Williard
Rockwell-former Chairman of Rockwell Int.). Their
success in warding off these takeover attempts probably
gave them a false sense of security.

These former takeover attempts were based on
stockholder votes rather than the cash takeover by
Hanson with the large (50%) premium. Against, this
arsenal, SCM had no defense.

Winners and Losers of the SCM Conglomerate Experience

As you review the past 20 years, it is easy to see
who the winners and losers were from the SCM
conglomerate experience.

The Winners

1.   The primary winner were the shareholders of Hanson Trust PLC.   They reaped the benefit of having the vast accumulated values of SCM transferred to them.

2.   SCM management were the next major beneficiaries with 23 managers receiving golden parachutes and watching their stock options rise dramatically.

3.   SCM stockholders who happened to buy the stock during the period from 1983 to 1985 and were lucky to be owning it when the takeover attempt was made.

The Losers

The primary losers were the stockholders of SCM Corporation who owned the shares during the acquisition period.   The GLidden shareholders, for example, never saw the $79 acquisition price made in May 1967 again. Even if they had, the $75 purchase price paid by Hanson was in dollars that bore no relationship to the purchasing power of the 1967 dollar.

Some Concluding Remarks and After Thoughts

On August 18, 1986, Hanson Trust announced the sale of the Glidden Pain unit to Imperial Chemical Industries for $580 million and was happy to report that it had already recouped $810 million of the $930 million dollar purchase price.   Hanson still holds the "Crown Jewel" the titanium dioxide pigment business, Smith Corona typewriters, Durkee Foods and some paper operations.   THe remaining businesses, effectively purchased for $120 million, will generate operating profits of at least $150 million in the current year, according to Hanson officials.

In December 3, 1986, article in the British newspaper The Times, Sir Gorden White, Chairman of Hanson Industries, the American arm of Hanson Trust justified takeovers when he stated "a major role played by takeovers is that of displacing unsuccessful managements and restoring the competitive position. Captains of yesterday's industries fight fiercely to preserve their areas of privilege and would rather go down with their ship than embrace inevitable change? The SCM management went down with the ship.

The SCM example clearly shows that the primary objective of a Chief Executive Officer should be to maximize shareholders wealth as clearly stated in Chapter 1 of every finance textbook. Maximizing shareholders wealth is not necessarily synonymous with growth in sales and earnings. If it were, the SCM Corporation would still be in tact today. The major problem with most conglomerate or multi-industry companies is that the stock market (the financial community) has not recognized the true value of these enterprises in the form of higher P/E ratios possibly because they are difficult to analyze and thus hard to understand. The low P/E ratios is what makes these companies vulnerable. The "takeover wave" of the 1980's, in my opinion, is a healthy occurrence and in spite of the criticism from the New York Stock Exchange and American Stock Exchange, is a process that should not be interfered with. Passing federal or state laws would only interfere with the free enterprise process that American business has enjoyed. The takeover wave is a healthy process that is going to keep the CEO's of the world's businesses on their toes. Stockholders meetings and stockholders votes have little or no relevance and have had little or no relevance for too long a time.

MANAGING A FIRST RATE INVESTMENT INTO A MAJOR CORPORATE DISASTER: THE EUROPEAN HEALTH SPAS STORY

by

Dr. Lawrence P. Huggins[1]

In 1966 U.S. Industries (USI) embarked upon an aggressive program to grow the company significantly and <u>rapidly</u>. The fundamentals of that growth program were based upon two elements: one of internal growth and one of growth through successful acquisition. The program of internal growth was seen as an effort to expand the existing USI companies within their own or into allied markets. However, right from the very beginning the prospects of significant internal growth were regarded by management as highly limited. When considered in light of the span of time needed to achieve meaningful participation in new markets and in light of the paucity of research and development going on within the company as a whole this, at the time, seemed a reasonable course of action. USI was in a hurry. With a few exceptions, it did not regard itself nor did it actually possess the scientific or engineering innovative capabilities that are attributable to such larger companies as General Electric, Dupont or AT & T. Philosophically, it regarded itself as a materials converter, not as an innovator. Accordingly, then, it chose to grow predominantly through a program of acquisitions.

Strategically, going the route of growth through acquisition was also consciously adopted as a substitute form of research and development. That is to say, it was viewed by USI corporate leadership as a way to obtain quick entry into, what for them were new markets and with the added benefit of having an entire cadre of experienced management in place.

The rate of growth was mindboggling. Starting with its initial acquisition during the latter part of 1966, U.S. industries succeeded in adding more than 90 medium sized companies to its family by 1969, a family which was to grow to 108 divisions by 1974. Imagine the enormity of an undertaking to acquire, and digest so much in such a short time! New products, new processes, wide geographical dispersion of facilities,

---

[1] Chairman of the Department of Management Sciences, Manhattan College and former President and CEO of U S Industries Agri-business group

new managers, new personnel, new union relationships, new markets including international customers, facilities, personnel, wholly owned channels of distribution, individualized and often bizarre divisional accounting and inventory control systems, and sitting on top of all this, a USI corporate staff which despite the presence of some individually brilliant managers was, essentially, unprepared either by training or experience to handle such breadth and diversity.

To help manage this complex new undertaking, the company was organized into 7 operating groups which, with the exceptions of the Apparel & Accessories Group and Service Business Group were designated on a regional basis. Thus, there came into being a Midwest Group, a Northeast Group, a Southern Group, a Western Group and an International Group. This arrangement of individual companies on a geographic basis rather than on an industry or family of companies basis proved to be a fundamental if not monumental error in organizational structuring. It unwittingly sacrificed operational, technical and market synergies for geographical proximity, ease of executive travel and even, in some cases, executive preferences for where they wished to live.

By 1974, this organizational aberration was discarded for a new group alignment which did indeed reorganize the operating divisions into a grouping of similar or related industries. In the process of the corporate reorganization and until a year or so after it was accomplished all of the seven group executive vice-presidents were replaced with only two remaining in the company in any capacity. The corporate officers of U.S. industries in New York City mirrored the extensive changes occurring in operations. Of eleven corporate officers reporting to the president and chairmen of the board, nine were removed from their positions. One of these was to survive for a while, and one retired. Only two of the originals, the vice-president and general counsel and the vice-president and corporate controller weathered the storm of reorganization repositioning. These latter, perhaps demonstrate that not the meek but the lawyers and accountants shall inherit the earth.

Nevertheless, and in spite of the cataclysmic changes caused by the ingestion of so many businesses, USI grew from a $108 million in industrial-oriented sales to a corporation which by 1973 was doing over $1.6 billion in a highly diversified variety of products and services. The corporation was well on its way to finding a position in every market segment in which it had an interest although still very far away from being a primary competitor in each of those markets.

From a strategic positioning point-of-view, U.S. industries wished to have a product portfolio which contained enough diversity that periodic down trends in one segment could be absorbed or even off-set in other segments and a product portfolio composed of companies which were or could reasonably be expected to become significant contenders in their markets. Specific acquisition strategy was to chose companies having a minimum annual sales volume of ten million dollars, pre-tax profits of 10%, a good cash flow and a strong return of investment. Included in the acquisition theory was insistence on the idea that the managers of the acquired companies be willing to stay on to continue their winning ways and that these executives, largely entrepreneurs, be willing to share in the give and take (or so it is said) corporate style of U.S. industries. This last, predictably enough, was a virtual contradiction of terms and in retrospect a demonstration of corporate naivete the top management of USI really thought that such a blending would occur.

But these entrepreneurs for the most part, were strong individuals with their own ideas and an almost physiological desire for personal freedom of action. The quid pro quo which USI believed it was offering to these companies was a partnership with a variety of financial and managerial resources which would help the newly acquired managements to each fulfill individual visions of their company's (now USI divisions) ultimate growth. USI also made these entrepreneurs millionaires in the buy-out process adding to their personal independence, and gave them typically, though not in every case, five year contingency contracts which paid each of them a high salary with the opportunity for large bonuses based on pre-tax profit performance and return on capital. By providing support in such areas as legal activities, tax reporting, economic studies, labor relations, insurance and public relations USI corporate leadership believed it would free the entrepreneurial juices of the acquired managers to flow. Thus, or so the theory went, these men could concentrate their energies on performing the work which they preferred and knew best: that of making, perfecting and selling the products which had already made them rich.

29

One of the more significant markets which U S Industries targeted for acquisition during this period was that of health. Based upon strong economic indicators of growing affluence and a expected increase in spending by consumers for both health and leisure products, the corporation entered both markets in 1968. During this year it enlarged its chain of retail optical stores and laboratories and entered the health spa business through acquisition of the European Health Spa Company which operated some sixty health spas around the country. During the course of the next nine years and until divestment, this number was to increase to 146 health spas operating in 28 states with particularly strong representation in California, New York/New Jersey, Virginia, Florida, and Georgia.

During the formative years of the health spa industry there was considerable uncertainty on the part of the public as to what constituted a health spa. A wide variety of businesses called themselves health spas. These ranged from massage parlors, old fashioned gyms and businesses offering "passive exercise" for weight reduction to multi-million interstate public corporations providing extensive gym, pool and sauna facilities. This lack of definition and identification created severe problems for both the public and management and it posed special problems for legislators since consumer problems arising in other modes, were often perceived as typical of all. This confusion was shared, for the most part, by USI corporate management. It had no previous knowledge or expertise in the health spa industry and save for a few executives who were forced by circumstances to learn more of the industry, top corporate management never did come to understand the business. This might have been acceptable had the corporate leadership followed its own philosophies and allowed the original entrepreneurs or their subsequent replacements to function with little interference in day-to-day operations. However that was not to be.

The foundation of a professional organizational, the association of physical fitness centers, by the leading companies in the health spa industry was undertaken. It was a reaction against the practices of some health spa operators, which were creating a climate confusing for potential consumers and injurious to the large body of health spa companies which conducted operations in business like manner. In addition to establishing a code of ethics for the industry, the association sought to define the industry. This was done in the association's brochure

#102, page 2 which described it as an industry "...composed of businesses or organizations promoting physical fitness and well being through major emphasis on the training in and use of exercise which may also offer, in addition, nutritional guidance and recreational and athletic activities."

The development of the industry was certainly timely. The United States was seen by many to be in the throes of an epidemic of massive proportions directed attributable to a lack of physical condition. Heart disease was accounting for nearly 250 deaths per 100,000 population with even cancer related deaths running significantly behind. For those in the 35-45 age group, an age group incidentally usually sufficiently affluent to pay for health club membership, heart disease was the leading cause of death among males. Dr. Henry L. Feffer, a leading orthopedic expert as reported in U.S. News and World Report, October 1975, page 2 estimated that 8 million people were suffering from chronic back conditions primarily related to a "...sedentary type of life..." by 1975, Americans were spending $155 billion for health care with the cost of health care, as reported in a Business Week article entitled "The Sky's the Limit On Health Care Costs," May 26, 1975, page 2 rising at a rate of 14% to 15 % annually. Further underscoring the timeliness of the emergence of exercise into a full-blown industry were powerful and significant statements of such organizations as the American Medical Association which noted that "exercise is the most significant factor contributing to the health of the individual." And "maintenance of a high physical activity level is an effective preventive against the development of coronary heart attack."

Of the major health spa companies then in existence, the European Health Spa Corporation was the largest and generally regarded by industry insiders as the most superior in facilities and programs. It had been put together earlier by a group, primarily composed of mormons who considered the body a living temple for God to dwell within. They had built or acquired the very best facilities available at the time. Accordingly, most of these facilities and equipment, housed usually in edifices with a Greek or Roman bath motif were the best currently available. Most typically, they utilized approximately 4000 to 8000 square feet and included an exercise floor with various types of resistance equipment, swimming pool, dry sauna, steam room, whirlpool, in some instances a eucalyptus room, tanning booths, health juice bar and, of course, showers and lockers. They were relatively plush and membership sales were brisk. Thus, in acquiring this company, U S Industries believed that it had succeeded in fulfilling all of its strategic acquisition standards: A company with solid cash flow, high profitability, experienced entrepreneurial leadership in place, the largest and best appointed facilities and, clearly, the recognized industry leader.

USI ownership was not absolute. They controlled 80% of the outstanding shares of common stock but there remained about a million and a half shares owned by some 2800 individual stockholders. While this, in itself, posed no special difficulties for day-to-day operations, it did create some expenditures that USI would later find to be onerous. More importantly, the major acquisition, along with several smaller spa company acquisitions was incorporated under the name of Health Industries Inc. Thus, its identity was somewhat schizophrenic. Within U S Industries, it was seen as health industries, an 80% owned subsidiary. To the public it was known as European Health Spas.

From the very beginning of the new corporate relationship, it was clear that the entrepreneurial style of management of the former owners and the USI requirements for operational budgeting, performance review and capital expenditure approval were in conflict. Senior European management resented what they saw as meddling into day-to-day operations by group management, corporate lawyers and internal auditors who lacked any knowledge of the health spa business. Many senior USI management, on the other hand, saw the health spa people as un-business-like fitness freaks who drove white Lincoln Continental "spa mobiles" and had more regard for the size of pectorals, biceps and triceps than they did for the serious conduct of a business.

This mutual distaste of management approaches might have been immaterial had spa operations continued to show the profit performance which initially attracted USI to acquire the business.

There is a seasonal rhythm to health spa membership sales. Typically, after Labor Day in September, membership sales become brisk and stay so until about the end of the first week of December. Sales then usually dip for about a month until the second week of January. From mid-January on until about mid-June, sales again are usually healthy. With

32

the on-set of summer and until after Labor Day, sales
volume goes down, sometimes drastically.   U S
Industries did not understand or appreciate these
rhythms.   It did not appreciate the reduced
profitability performance and it did not appreciate the
"spa mobiles" and high sales bonus participation
practices of European's management. Corporate control
contacts, especially auditing, increased.   These
resulted in the exposure of a number of management
practices and conflicts of interest which caused the
already alienated USI management to fire most of
European's senior managers. The aftermath of this was
a convoluted series of suits and counter suits which
dragged on for a number of years and which were
ultimately settled out of court.   But that's another
story.

    In the absence of well constructed communications
explaining the dismissals,the dismissed senior health
spa management were followed out by resignations of
many middle managers and the company left in
considerable disarray.   To turn the now decimated
company around, USI appointed one of its excellent
corporate managers to the presidency of the division
and assigned several corporate legal and accounting
types to spend <u>part</u> of their time assisting him. His
efforts were prodigious and he might have succeeded.
However, with intensified corporate surveillance,
coupled with requirements for his frequent personal
presence in New York, and his own admitted lack of
industry knowledge, progress was slow. Sales volume
continued to drop and USI was in a hurry. Thus, after
a frustrating year or so, this executive and USI parted
company.

    The number two man of one of the larger spa chain
competitors was recruited to fill the vacant
presidency. While not a mormon like the earlier group
of managers, he did seem to possess appropriate
operational credentials and was capable, so he said, of
attracting other experienced managers to fill the
vacancies left by the massive dismissal and/or
defection of the first group of managers. True to his
word, this new president recruited key vice-presidents
and middle managers and, with the permission of USI,
restructured the corporate organization.

    Costs began to increase as European's corporate
staff ballooned to sixteen vice-presidents. However,
sales volume increased dramatically, almost from the
very beginning of the new leadership and profitability
seemed to return.

In New York at this time, USI's corporate staff was undergoing its own upheavals. Its president assumed the chairmanship and the office of the presidency became a revolving door. During one year between 1973 and mid 1974, in what looked like the machinations of a praetorian guard replacing Roman emperors, four different individuals held the office. While these corporate politics were being played out, relatively little attention was given to the health spa business by New York management, and it was beginning to show losses again.

In mid-1974, C.R. Luigs was appointed president of U S Industries. A vigorous, perhaps brilliant individual, he immediately took control of all the operations and quickly became convinced that something fundamental was wrong in health industries. He dispatched a series of managers to find out. Millions of dollars of member contract sales which had been reported in the year of the sale, but which were for multi-year memberships were the problem. Booked totally in one year for services to be provided in subsequent years, they tended to inflate profits in the year the contract was issued. This was acceptable accounting practice at that time and, from a management point of view ok as long as sales volume remained high and payments on the contracts-overwhelmingly financed over 24 to 48 month time periods-were kept up by the members. That was the fundamental error! Not only was there a high incidence of failure to make payments, but member contracting standards were so loosely devised that a number of unscrupulous sales people were able to obtain large sales bonuses for exceeding sales budgets often with contracts which were improperly drawn. In one case, a salesman was found to have enrolled his dog.

Needless to say, there was another drastic management turnover. Under its fourth new president, health industries succeeded in detecting and writing off to bad debt all of the uncollectible contracts. Restructuring took place with considerable cost reduction and thinning out of corporate staff. Young, ambitious sales vice-presidents were found from among the effective middle managers and put in charge of challenging sales budgets. Member contract requirements were revised and contract review control procedures installed. An independent internal audit team was constituted and an operational quality control system installed. With the assistance of academic consultants, new fitness programs were developed and an aggressive marketing program launched.

All of this, and more, succeeded and the company experienced several years of modest but growing profits. However, USI was having problems with its largest single business and transferred health's president to that operation in the hope that it too could be as swiftly and dramatically turned around. In his place they chose to put a financial man to serve as an interim president. This interregnum lasted for two years during which time every one of the young operational vice-presidents quit. The interregnum president was clearly not a people person in a people oriented business and sales again began to drop-off precipitously. Ultimately, the two year temporary president was replaced leaving behind a wounded and bleeding company. A new executive was recruited from a non-health spa but consumer oriented business to serve as the sixth president in nine years. As it turned out, he was the last for U S Industries, sorely pressed for new capital investment to replace aging and depreciated plant and equipment elsewhere was forced to keep health industries afloat by underwriting operational losses to the tune of over a million dollars a month. USI was also bleeding without viable management alternatives, USI virtually gave the business away in 1981 to those competitors who were willing take over customer commitments by health spas open under new management.

This paper started with a title: Managing a first rate investment into a major corporate disaster: the European health spas story. Acquisition disasters rarely occur suddenly. In this case the whole drama was acted out in a 13 year time period. When did the disaster start to take place? My answer would be that it had started before the ink was dry on the original acquisition deal.

SUSTAINABLE GROWTH AND BUSINESS COMBINATIONS

by

John J. Clark, Margaret T. Clark and Gerald Olson[1]

In the context of managing growth, the question of an appropriate growth rate over a defined time frame takes the form: "What rate of growth is sustainable vis-a-vis the financial profile of the firm, the productivity of factor inputs, and the dividend payout policy. Stated differently, if the productivity of factor inputs is held constant, what percentage increase in sales can be maintained without necessitating a change in financial policy? If sales grow at a higher rate, the firm can exercise a combination of options to finance the increment in total sales: increase debt, reduce dividend payout, or issue equity securities. Each option alters established financial policies. On the other hand, if the productivity of factor inputs could be increased, improved operating performance would generate higher profit margins which at a constant dividend payout would favorably affect retained earnings. Thus, while the models presented in this paper have a primarily financial orientation, they incorporate an important, underlying technological component.

However, management must recognize the distinction between sustainable growth and optimal growth. The two can coincide but may diverge. The objective of management is to maximize the market value of the common stock. This is achieved when the required return of the stock -- the return reflecting the risk posture of the firm -- equates to the actual return on the common stock, and the financial structure minimizes the weighted average cost of capital. The common shareholders are receiving a return commensurate with the risk of their investment. Under these conditions, the sustainable rate of growth would be optimal (other factors constant). If the actual rate of growth and the sustainable rate of growth were also identical, then both would be optimal. However, the sustainable growth rate may be the product of a sub-optimal financial structure. In this event a revised financial

---

[1] Respectively Director, Graduate Studies of Business Administration, Drexel University; Professor of Finance Villanova University, and Associate Professor of Finance LaSalle University

policy might minimize the cost of capital and concurrently optimize sustainable growth, achieve a preferred risk-return equilibrium, and higher market value for the common stock. The question of the relationship between firm valuation, sustainable growth, and the risk-return trade off is beyond the scope of our present enquiry.

The Higgins' Model

In 1977 and 1981, Robert C. Higgins demonstrated that the financial policies of many corporations may be at variance with their growth objectives. [11, 12] As a guide for setting compatible financial policies and growth objectives, Higgins' developed a formula to calculate a rate of sustainable growth. In deriving his formula, Higgins made the following assumptions:

1 - Book depreciation is adequate to recapture the value of existing assets;

2 - Profit margin (P) on new sales (S_1) correspond to that of existing sales (S_0); hence the change in sales ($\triangle S$) equals $S_1 - S_0$;

3 - The firm has an established financial-structure (L) without the sale of new common stock. The financial structure is the total of all debt and equities financing current and long term assets;

4 - The firm has an established dividend payout rate (D); thus the target retention ratio is (1 - D);

5 - New fixed assets (F) at book value represent a stated proportion of the change in physical volume of output (real sales);

6 - New current assets (C) are a stated proportion of sales in nominal dollars;

7 - Sales at the beginning of the period are represented by (S_0) and the projected sales during the period by (S_1);

8 - T denotes the ratio of total assets to net sales, and the ratio is constant for new and existing sales;

9 - Firm will rely on retained earnings for equity financing, and new common stock will not be issued.

Based on these assumptions, Higgins describes the derivation of the basic formula:

... P and T are the same for new sales as for existing sales, the new assets required to support increased sales are forecast to be ΔS (T).

... On the other side of the balance sheet, total profits for the year are expected to be $(S+\Delta S)P$ and additions to retained earnings to be $(S+\Delta S)P(1-D)$...because every \$1 added to retained earnings enables the company to borrow \$L without increasing its debt to equity ratio ... new borrowings should equal $(S +\Delta S)P(E - D)L$. [10]

Since assets must equal liabilities plus equity, additions to assets must be covered by an increase in retained earnings and new debt. Setting the two quantities equal and solving for $\Delta S/S_0$ yields Expression 1:

$$g* = \frac{\Delta S}{S_0} = \frac{P(1-D)(1+L)}{T-\{P(1-D)(1+L)\}} \qquad (1)$$

Appendix I presents the consolidated statements of the Burroughs Corporation for 1980 and 1981. These form the basic data to illustrate the calculations of sustainable growth under conditions of stable prices, rising and falling prices, and with or without the imposition of a corporate income tax. Exhibit I puts the Burroughs data on a pre-tax basis and Exhibit II lists the post-tax data. Both Exhibits display the relevant variables in the models discussed.

Case I-Higgins' Model: Stable Prices and No Corporate Income Tax

Taking the data from Exhibit I and using Expression I,

$$g* = \frac{.0746(1-.426)(1+1.036)}{1.304-[.0746(1-.574)(1+1.036)]}$$

$$= .0716478 \quad \text{or} \quad 7.16\% \text{ (rounded)}$$

Unless the actual growth rate equals the sustainable growth rate $(g*)$, the firm will have to reassess its financial policies. Thus, if $g > g*$, the firm

EXHIBIT I
Burroughs Corporation
Consolidated Income Statement
1981 Dollars Before Taxes
(Thousands of Dollars)

		1981
Total Revenue		$3,405,428
Less		
Operating Cost		3,006,224
Earnings Before Interest & Taxes		$ 399,204
Less		
Interest Expense		145,078
Earnings Before Taxes		$ 254,126

Shares Outstanding	=	41,641,000
Dividends Per Share	=	$2.60
Net-Income Per Share (EPS)	=	$6.103
Profit Margin (P)	=	.0746
Dividend Payout Ratio (D)	=	.426
Retention Ratio (1-D)	=	.574
Total Assets/Sales (T)	=	1.304
Financial Structure (L) -		
Total Debt/Equity	=	1.036
Current Assets/Current Sales (C)	=	.676
Fixed Assets/Sales (F)	=	.446
Price Trend (J)	=	+.09/-.09
Net-Working Capital/Sales (W)	=	.279801
Long Term Debt to Equity (L_L)	=	.3689508

might have to seek additional financing through a higher retention ratio and/or by sale of debt or equity securities. Conversely, if $g < g^*$, the company may have excess capital relative to investment needs and may increase dividends, reduce leverage or increase liquid assets. [10]

Case II-Higgins' Model: Rising Prices and No Corporate Income Tax

Expression 1 can be modified to allow for price increases or decreases. This yields Expression 2,

$$g^* = \frac{\Delta S}{S_0} = \frac{[(1=J)P((1-D)(1+L)] \quad -JC}{[(1+J)C+F]-[(1+J)P(1-D)(1+L)J]} \quad (2)$$

Taking the data from Exhibit I, a 9 percent price rise (J), we have:

$g^* = .0291144$ or 2.91% (rounded)

Case III-Higgins' Model: Declining Prices and No Corporate Income Tax

Utilizing Expression 2 and the data from Exhibit I, we have:

$g^* = \dfrac{.1401759}{1.0683002} = .131214$ or 13.12% (rounded)

Although we cannot fully discuss the impact of price changes on sustainable growth without taking into account the tax factor, it is obvious that the effect of price increases or decreases on sustainable growth in a particular company must depend on: (a) the degree which price variations affect specific revenue and expense items; (b) the mix of fixed and variable costs; and (c) whether the annual depreciation is sufficient to maintain the replacement value of existing assets. Based upon his research on U.S. manufacturing in 1974, Higgins concluded that:

> Roughly speaking, the real sustainable growth rate declines by 2.2% for every 5 percentage point increase in the inflation rate. With approximate 10% inflation rate in 1974, real sustainable growth falls from an inflation-free 10.5% to 6.1%. For comparison, the actual real growth in manufacturing sales in 1974 was 3.8 percent, while figures for the prior two years were 8.2% and 8.4%. [12]

Descending from the macro view to the individual firm, the effects of price level changes are really indeterminate. For example, if for a particular company at a given quantity of output, revenues rose faster than costs, then the following scenario might unfold:

-- an improved profit margin (P);
-- assuming higher interest rates, an increase in the cost of capital;
-- depreciation charges inadequate to cover the cost of replacement assets;
-- debt repayment in cheaper real dollars (L);
-- pressure to raise dividend payouts (D);
-- higher inventory investment costs;
-- a rachet effect to higher tax brackets.

Conversely, if expenses increased faster than revenues, some or all of the following might occur:
-- lower profit margins (P) perhaps negative earnings:
-- assuming falling interest rates, a lower cost of capital;
-- depreciation charges in excess of replacement cost of equipment;
-- debt repayment in higher real dollar values;
-- a lower dividend payout (D) ratio and higher retention ratio (1 - D);
-- lower inventory investment costs;
-- a drop to lower tax brackets or accumulation of tax loss carryover.

The reader can easily outline similar sequences of events to cover the phenomenon of a falling price level. Two conclusions are readily apparent, however: (1) a computer model of the firm would be necessary to forecast the impact of rising or falling price levels on the nominal sustainable growth of the firm; (2) the computer model with equal ease could adjust for price changes and project real sustainable growth of the firm.

Case IV-Higgins' Model: Stable Prices; After Taxes

Utilizing the data from Exhibit II and Expression 1, we have:

$$g* = \frac{P(1-D)(1+L)}{T-[P(1-D)(1+L)]} \tag{1}$$

$$= .0188389 \quad \text{or } 1.88\% \text{ (rounded)}$$

EXHIBIT II
Burroughs Corporation
Consolidated Income Statement
1981 Dollars Before Taxes
(Thousands of Dollars)

	1981
Total Revenue	$3,405,428
Less	
Operating Cost	3,006,224
Earnings Before Interest & Taxes	$ 399,204
Less	
Interest Expense	145,078
Earnings Before Taxes	$ 254,126
Less	
Taxes (58.6%)	105,200
Earnings After Taxes	$ 148,926
Less	
Dividends	108,540
Addition to Retained Earnings	$ 40,386

Shares Outstanding	=	41,641,000
Dividends Per Share	=	$2.60
Net-Income Per Share (EPS)	=	$3.58
Profit Margin (P)	=	.0437
Dividend Payout Ratio (D)	=	.729
Retention Ratio (1-D)	=	.271
Total Assets/Sales (T)	=	1.304
Financial Structure (L) -		
Total Debt/Equity	=	1.036
Current Assets/Current Sales (C)	=	.676
Fixed Assets/Sales (F)	=	.446
Price Trend (J)	=	+.09/-.09
Net-Working Capital/Sales (W)	=	.279801
Long Term Debt to Equity (L_L)	=	.3689508

Case V-Higgins' Model: Rising Prices; After Taxes

Combining the data from Exhibit II with Expression 2, we have;

$$g* = \frac{[(1=J)P((1-D)(1+L)] \quad -JC}{[(1+J)C+F]-[(1+J)P(1-D)(1+L)J]} \qquad (2)$$

$$= -.0292748 \quad \text{or} \quad -2.93\% \quad \text{(rounded)}$$

Case VI-Higgins' Model: Falling Prices; After Taxes

In this case, a 9 percent decline in price is inserted into Expression 2:

$$g* = .0778657 \quad \text{or} \quad 7.79\% \quad \text{(rounded)}$$

The effect of the imposition of a corporate income tax is consistent at all price levels. Sustainable growth is sharply reduced by the tax bite.

The Johnson's Model

Johnson qualified the original Higgins' model and the presumption of a constant _financial_ structure. [13]. The former hinged the discussion on the rate of sustainable growth using a constant _capital_ structure [long term debt to equity (L_L)]. Based upon Higgins' assumptions, Johnson shows that total uses of funds are composed of the change in total nominal _current_ assets, $[(S + \triangle S)(1 + J) - S]C$ plus _new nominal fixed assets_, $(\triangle S)F$. Sources of funds equal the increase in nominal debt plus retained earnings, $(S+\triangle S)(1 + J)P(1-D)(1+ L)$. However, Johnson by focusing on capital structure (long term debt to equity) allows working capital to float with nominal sales. The revised real sustainable rate of growth thus takes the form:

$$g_R = \frac{\triangle S}{S} = \frac{Y(1+J)-WJ}{F-[(1+J)Y]+[W(1+J)]} \qquad (3)$$

where, $Y = P(1 - D)(1 + L_L)$

and $W = $ the ratio of nominal net working capital to nominal sales.

Case I-Johnson's Model: Stable Prices; No Taxes

Utilizing the data from Exhibit I in Expression 3, we have:

$$Y = .0746(1 - .426)(1 + .3689508)$$

$$= .0589619$$

Then, the real sustainable growth (g_R) under Johnson's methodology becomes:

$$g_R = \frac{.0589313(1+0) - (0)(.279801)}{.446-[(1+0).0589313]+[.279801(1+0)]}$$

$$= .08837 \text{ or } 8.84\% \text{ (rounded)}$$

This compares to a sustainable growth rate of 7.16 percent under the Higgins' Model.

Case II-Johnson's Model: Rising Prices; No Taxes

Inserting the 9 percent price increase into Expression 3, we have:

$$g_R = \frac{.0390531}{.6867479} = .0568667 \text{ or } 5.69\% \text{ (rounded)}$$

Note that Y, once calculated is a constant.

Case III-Johnson's Model: Declining Prices; No Taxes

$$g_R = \frac{.0788374}{.6469636} = .1218576 \text{ or } 12.1\% \text{ (rounded)}$$

Case IV-Johnson's Model: Stable Prices; After Taxes

With introduction of the corporate income tax, Y must be recalculated:

$$Y = .0437 (1 - .729)(1 + .3689508)$$

$$= .016212$$

Then, from Exhibit II and Expression 3:

$$g_R = \frac{.0162123(1+0) - (0)(.279801)}{.446-[(1+0).016212]+[.27980(1+0)]}$$

$$= .0228471 \text{ or } 2.28\% \text{ (rounded)}$$

Case V-Johnson's Model: Rising Prices; After Taxes

Introducing an upward trend in prices of 9 percent into Expression 3 downgrades sustainable growth:

$$g_R = \frac{.0162123(1+.09) - (.09)(.279801)}{.446-[(1+.09).016212]+[.27980(1+.09)]}$$

$$= -.0102425 \text{ or } -1.02\% \text{ (rounded)}$$

Case VI-Johnson's Model: Declining Prices; After Taxes

Once again tax effects and declining prices can combine to affect positively sustainable growth. Assuming a downward trend in prices of 9 percent,

$$g_R = \frac{.0162123(1-.09) - (-.09)(.279801)}{.446-[(1-.09).016212]+[.27980(1-.09)]}$$

$$= .0582257 \text{ or } 5.82\% \text{ (rounded)}$$

Summary and Comparison

Table I presents a comparison of the Burrough's results using the Higgin's and Johnson's Models.

Table 1

	Higgin's Model ($g*$)	Johnson's Model (g_R)
Before Taxes		
Stable Prices	7.16%	8.84%
Rising Prices	2.91%	5.69%
Declining Prices	13.12%	12.19%
After Taxes		
Stable Prices	1.88%	2.28%
Rising Prices	2.93%	-1.02%
Declining Prices	7.79%	5.82%

The reader will recall the essential difference between the models lies in the assumption of a constant financial structure by Higgins and a constant capital structure by Johnson. The latter allows for the effects of period price changes on current assets and current liabilities. Thus in a period of rising prices, with a constant capital structure, the sustainable growth is higher than that attainable were the firm to adhere to an established financial structure.

On the other hand, in both cases (a target financial structure or a target capital structure), the sustainable growth rate is lower than that attainable under conditions of price stability. The reason for this phenomenon lies in the historical cost financial statements used to describe financial or capital structures and to set target ratios. It follows that

46

in the face of persistent inflation management can maintain a stable capital structure over time only by using a constant dollar debt/equity ratio or one based upon market values.

Similar reasoning explains the behavior of sustainable growth in periods of declining prices. In both models, sustainable growth exceeds that obtainable under conditions of stable prices but the sustainable growth rate from the Higgins' Model exceeds that of the Johnson's model. Again, the phenomenon is attributable to the price effects on net-working capital incorporated in Johnson's model.

Both the Higgins's and Johnson's models escape the problem of optimal sustainable growth by implicitly assuming the firm has achieved an optimal financial or capital structure.

Business Combinations and Sustainable Growth

The variables incorporated in the Higgins' and Johnson's models obviously are pertinent to the design of the financial and/or capital structures of the combinations. The financial and/or capital structure reflects the type and kind of consideration paid to the stockholders of the acquired company and the accounting method (purchase or pooling) used to record the transaction.[2] For example, if the Burroughs Corporation were financed entirely with common stock, the sustainable rate of growth after taxes in 1981 would rise to 2.91%; if the financial structure were 50 percent debt and 50 percent common, the sustainable growth rate would approximate 2.88%. These compare to a sustainable growth rate of 1.88% based upon 1981 debt/equity ratio of 1.036.

Appendix II contains a sample of 35 business combinations selected from the 1965-1970 merger wave and the current, continuing merger wave from 1977. Twenty-one cases fell into the first period and 14 cases in the second period. For each combination in

---

[2] The accounting rules have changed over the past two decades. Combinations put together in the 1960's were subject to ARB 48. Under ARB 48, the liberal interpretation of the pooling provisions allowed almost any combination to be recorded as a pooling. APB 16, 17, and 18 adopted in 1970 and 1971 set tighter criteria for distinguishing between purchase and pooling as well as the treatment of goodwill.[1,2]

the sample, sustainable growth was calculated six to eight months prior to the combination; at the time of the combination, sustainable growth was calculated on the basis of the pro-forma consolidated financial statements. The cases selected were those with only the major combination in the year under study although a minor combination (less than 10 percent of the acquiring firm's size) was tolerated.

Of the 35 combinations in the sample, 16 showed a higher sustainable growth rate (calculated by the Higgins' model) compared to the pre-acquisition rates of the independent entities. In 19 combinations, the sustainable growth rate dropped below pre-acquisition levels. Of the 19 combinations with lower sustainable growth rates, the calculated sustainable growth rate in 15 cases located in the range set by the minimum and maximum rates of the companies in their pre-acquisition status.

There were 21 poolings; 9 associated with higher post-acquisition sustainable growth rates and 12 with lower post-acquisition growth rates. Fourteen purchase transactions were recorded; eight with higher sustainable growth rates and 6 with lower sustainable growth rates. The literature tends to assert that when market values exceed book values, pooling is the preferred option; and when book values exceed market values, the purchase option is the preferred strategy. [3, 6]

However, based upon our preliminary survey, we cannot conclude that either accounting option tends to facilitate a higher sustainable growth rate. Other variables present in the individual case apparently offset the accounting options, based upon the nature of the consideration paid, does impact the financial and/or capital structure and thus sustainable growth. If the latter concept were properly incorporated into the financial planning of the combination, it may well serve to reduce post-acquisition adjustments to the financial and/or debt structure and enhance the prospects of a successful combination.

In this respect, the proportion of successful business combinations does not inspire confidence. Based upon the literature, we might assert with equal certainty that business combinations have, on balance, yielded neutral or negative returns to stockholders of the acquiring firms, that half or more of the combinations fail to meet expectations or result in financial losses to the shareholders of the acquiring firm; and that one of six mergers fails outright. [4] Mueller, after an extensive survey of the empirical literature, stated:

> ...the empirical literature draws a surprisingly consistent picture. Whatever the stated or unstated goals of managers are, the mergers they have consummated, on the average, not generated extra profits for the acquiring firms, and have not resulted in increased efficiency. [14]

Summary

Applied to mergers and acquisitions, the sustainable growth rate constitutes a valuable tool in the construction of a business combination.

1 - It can assist in the evaluation of a target company. If the target company has a low sustainable growth rate, the acquiring firm must be prepared to insert new resources or drain-off its existing resources to support the target. If the latter, then the sustainable growth rate of the buyer will decline. This assumes the objective of the combination is to raise or maintain the existing actual growth rates. [8].

2 - The nature and the amount of the consideration to consummate the transaction affects the component variables of sustainable growth. Payment of excessive premiums for the target company (as in the DuPont-Conoco and Texas-Geddy cases) can reduce sustainable and trigger a sell-off of assets to reorganize the financial and/or capital structure.

3 - An awareness of the sustainable growth concept in the planning stage should affect the type and kind of consideration paid as well as the choice of available tax options.

4 - Estimation of a feasible sustainable growth rate may even deter combinations with marginal probabilities for success. In addition, if the planners posit a desired growth rate, they can reverse the formulae to design an appropriate financial and/or capital structure. [5]

REFERENCES

1 - Accounting Principles Board (APB), OMNIBUS OPINION, 1966, American Institute of Certified Public Accountants (AICPA), 1967.

... Opinion No. 16, BUSINESS COMBINATIONS, 1970, AICPA, 1970.
... Opinion No. 17, INTANGIBLE ASSETS, 1970, AICPA, 1970.
... Opinion No. 18, THE EQUITY METHOD OF ACCOUNTING FOR INVESTMENTS IN COMMON STOCK, 1971, AICPA, 1971.
... Opinion No. 23, ACCOUNTING FOR INCOME TAXES-SPECIAL AREAS, 1972, AICPA, 1972.
... Opinion No. 24, ACCOUNTING FOR INCOME TAXES-INVESTMENTS IN COMMON STOCK ACCOUNTED FOR BY THE EQUITY METHOD, 1972, AICPA, 1972.
... Opinion No. 28, INTERIN FINANCIAL REPORTING, 1973, AICPA, 1973.
... Opinion No. 29, ACCOUNTING FOR NON-MONETARY TRANSACTIONS, 1973, AICPA, 1973.
... Opinion No. 30, REPORTING THE RESULTS OF OPERATIONS, 1973, AICPA, 1973.

2 - AICPA, ACCOUNTING RESEARCH BULLETIN, No. 48, BUSINESS COMBINATIONS, January 1957.

3 - Anderson, John C. and Joseph G. Lounderback III, "Income Manipulation and Purchase-Pooling: Some Additional Results," JOURNAL OF ACCOUNTING RESEARCH, Autumn 1973, pp. 338-343.

4 - Clark, John J., BUSINESS MERGER AND ACQUISITIONS STRATEGIES, Englewood Cliffs, New Jersey: Prentice-Hall, Inc., 1985.

5 - Clark, John J., Margaret T. Clark, and Andrew Verzilli, "Strategic Planning and Sustainable Growth," THE COLUMBIA JOURNAL OF WORLD BUSINESS, Fall 1985, pp. 47-51.

6 - Copeland, Ronald M. and Joseph F. Wojdak, "Income Manipulation and the Purchase-Pooling Choice,k" JOURNAL OF ACCOUNTING RESEARCH, Autumn 1969, pp. 188-195.

7 - Financial Accounting Standards Board, ACCOUNTING FOR BUSINESS COMBINATIONS AND PURCHASED INTANGIBLES, August 19, 1976.

8 -   Fruhan, William E., "How Fast Should a Company
       Grow?" HARVARD BUSINESS REVIEW, N.D., pp. 84-93.

9 -   Govindarajan, V. and J.K. Shank, "Cash
       Sufficiency: The Missing Link in Strategic
       Planning," CORPORATE ACCOUNTING, N.D., pp. 23-31.

10-   Higgins, Robert, "Sustainable Growth: New Tool in
       Bank Lending," JOURNAL OF COMMERCIAL LENDING, June
       1977, pp. 47-58.

11-   Higgins, Robert, "How Much Growth Can A Firm
       Afford," FINANCIAL MANAGEMENT, Fall 1977, pp. 7-
       15.

12-   Higgins, Robert, "Sustainable Growth Under
       Inflation," FINANCIAL MANAGEMENT, Fall 1981, pp.
       36-40.

13-   Johnson, Dana, "The Behavior of Financial
       Structure and Sustainable Growth in An
       Inflationary Environment," FINANCIAL MANAGEMENT,
       Autumn 1981, pp. 30-35.

14-   Mueller, Dennis C., "The Effects of Conglomerate
       Mergers: A Survey of the Empirical Evidence,"
       JOURNAL OF BANKING AND FINANCE, Vol. 1, 1977, p.
       339.

Appendix 1

Consolidated Financial Statements

Burroughs Corporation
1980-1981

Burroughs Corporation
(Thousands of Dollars)
After Taxes

	1981	1980	Increase(+) Decrease(-) Over 1980
Total Revenues	$3,405,428	$2,902,356	+
Less Operating Costs	3,006,224	2,686,611	+
Earnings Before Interest & Taxes	$ 339,204	$ 215,745	+
Less Interest Expense	145,078	81,373	+
Earnings Before Taxes	$ 254,126	$ 134,372	+
Less Taxes(58.6%)(39%)	105,200	52,400	+
Earnings After Taxes	$ 148,926	$ 81,972	+
Less Dividends	108,540	107,501	+
Addition to Retained Earnings	$ 40,386	($25,529)	+

Burroughs Corporation

Consolidated Balance Sheet
(Thousands of Dollars)

Current Assets	1981	1980	Increase (+) Decrease (−) Over 1980
Cash	$ 9,065	$ 23,370	−
Short Term Investments	46,028	35,113	+ 10,915
Accounts and Notes Receivable, net	1,052,433	906,637	+
Inventories			
Finished Equipment, supplies and accessories	691,455	554,939	+
Work in Process	383,477	417,068	−
Prepaid taxes and other	119,878	96,834	+
Total Current Assets	$2,302,306	$2,033,961	+
Long-Term Receivables, net	$385,730	$349,366	+
Rental Equipment and Related Inventories	$1,628,777	$1,524,500	+
Less: Accumulated Depreciation	716,624	$ 693,532	+
Net	$ 912,153	$ 830,968	+
Properties			
Less: Accumulated Depreciation	453,772	402,878	+
Net	$ 606,178	517,381	+
Other Assets	$ 233,033	123,018	+
Total Assets	$ 4,439,400	$ 3,854,694	+

Burroughs Corporation

Consolidated Balance Sheet
continued
(Thousands of Dollars)

	1981	1980	Increase (+) Decrease (−) Over 1980
Current Liabilities			
Notes Payable	$ 397,442	$ 513,910	−
Current Maturities of Long Term Debt	31,343	106,548	−
Accounts Payable	397,104	270,641	+
Accrued Payrolls & Commissions	163,752	107,922	+
Accrued Taxes other than Income Taxes	69,408	66,379	+
Customers' Deposits & Prepayments	154,893	155,685	−
Dividends Payable	27,681	26,982	+
Estimated Income Taxes	110,531	18,800	+
Total Current Liabilities	$1,352,154	$1,266,867	+
Deferred Income Taxes	$ 102,829	$ 90,346	+
Long Term Debt	$ 804,341	$ 372,455	+
Shareholders' Equity			
Common Stock ($5 par)	$ 210,317	$ 207,756	−
Paid-in Capital	448,144	436,041	+
Retained Earnings	1,522,030	1,481,644	+
Treasury Stock (41,000 Shares at Cost)	(415)	(415)	0
Total Equity	$2,180,076	$2,125,026	+
Total Liabilities and Equity	$4,439,400	$3,854,694	+

APPENDIX II

SUSTAINABLE GROWTH SELECTED

BUSINESS COMBINATIONS

1965 to 1970 and 1977 to 1986

(HIGGINS' MODEL)

SUSTAINABLE GROWTH IN BUSINESS
COMBINATIONS

Company A: American Hospital Supply, Inc.;
Company B: Haemonetics Corp.
Date of Combination: 1983
Method of Accounting: Pooling

Pre-Acquisition Sustainable Growth: Rate:

Company A: American Hospital Supply, In.   14.96%
Company B: Haemonetics Corp.   13.50%
Post-Combination Sustainable Growth: 12.89%

Company A: Anaconda
Company B: ARCO
Date of Combination: 1977
Method of Accounting: Purchase

Pre-Acquisition Sustainable Growth: Rate:

Company A: Anaconda   7.29%
Company B: ARCO   10.41%
Post-Combination Sustainable Growth: 6.58%

Company A: Armour & Co.
Company B: Baldwin-Lima-Hamilton
Date of Combination: 1965
Method of Accounting: Pooling

Pre-Acquisition Sustainable Growth   Rate:

Company A: Armour & Co.   6.95%
Company B: Baldwin-Lima-Hamilton   14.95%
Post-Combination Sustainable Growth: 1.98%

Company A: Avon Products, Inc.
Company B: Tiffany & Co.
Date of Combination: 1979
Method of Accounting: Pooling

Pre-Acquisition Sustainable Growth   Rate:

Company A: Avon Products, Inc.   12.12%
Company B: Tiffany & Co.   8.94%
Post-Combination Sustainable Growth   11.04%

Company A: Bausch & Lomb, Inc.
Company B: Charles River Breeding Laboratories, Inc.
Date of Combination: 1983
Method of Accounting: Pooling

Pre-Acquisition Sustainable Growth:	Rate:
Company A: Bausch & Lomb, Inc.	4.56%
Company B: Charles River Breeding Laboratories, Inc.	9.47%
Post-Combination Sustainable Growth:	9.41%

Company A: Beatrice Foods Co.
Company B: E. R. Moore Co.
Date of Combination: 1969
Method of Accounting: Pooling

Pre-Acquisition Sustainable Growth	Rate:
Company A: Beatrice Foods	9.76%
Company B: E. R. Moore	7.76%
Post-Acquisition Sustainable Growth	9.06%

Company A: Brown Co.
Company B: KVP Sutherland Paper Co.
Date of Combination: 1966
Method of Accounting: Pooling

Pre-Acquisition Sustainable Growth:	Rate:
Company A: Brown Co.	1.57%
Company B: KVP Sutherland Paper Co.	2.73%
Post-Combination Sustainable:	2.66%

Company A: Caterpillar Tractor
Company B: Townmotor Corp.
Date of Combination: 1965
Method of Accounting: Pooling

Pre-Acquisition Sustainable Growth:	Rate:
Company A: Caterpillar Tractor Co.	18.87%
Company B: Townmotor Corp.	14.40%
Post-Combination Sustainable Growth	18.67%

Company A: Certain-Teed Corp.
Company B: Gustin-Bacon-Manufacturing Co.
Date of Combination: 1966
Method of Accounting: Pooling

Pre-Acquisition Sustainable Growth   Rate:

Company A: Certain-Teed Corp.   4.76%
Company B: Gustin-Bacon Manufacturing Co.   4.31%
Post-Acquisition Sustainable Growth: 1.73%

Company A: Cross Co.
Company B: Kearney & Trecker
Date of Combination: 1979
Method of Accounting: Pooling

Pre-Acquisition Sustainable Growth: Rate:

Company A: Cross Co.   16.35%
Company B: Kearney & Trecker   12.93%
Post-Combination Sustainable Growth: 14.67%

Company A: Diebold, Inc.
Company B: Lamson Corp.
Date of Combination: 1965
Method of Accounting:Purchase

Pre-Acquisition Sustainable Growth: Rate:

Company A: Diebold, Inc.   9.85%
Company B: Lamson Corp.   5.21%
Post-Combination Sustainable Growth: 11.19%

Company A: Dun & Bradstreet Corp.
Company B: A. C. Nielsen Co.
Date of Combination: 1984
Method of Accounting: Pooling

Pre-Acquisition Sustainable Growth: Rate:

Company A: Dun & Bradstreet Corp.   15.89%
Company B: A. C. Neilsen Co.   16.07%
Post-Acquisition Sustainable Growth   10.54%

Company A: DuPont
Company B: Conoco
Date of Acquisition: 1982
Method of Accounting:Purchase

Pre-Acquisition Sustainable Growth:	Rate:
Company A: DuPont	5.12%
Company B: Conoco	16.40%
Post-Combination Sustainable Growth:	2.76%

Company A: Federal-Mogul Corp.
Company B: Sterling Aluminum Products, Inc.
Date of Combination: 1965
Method of Accounting: Pooling

Pre-Acquisition Sustainable Growth:	Rate:
Company A: Federal-Mogul Corp.	8.94%
Company B: Sterling Aluminum Products, Inc.	0.64%
Post-Combination Sustainable Growth:	5.51%

Company A: H. J. Heinz Co.
Company B: Ore-Ida Foods,Inc.
Date of Combination: 1965
Method of Accounting: Pooling

Pre-Acquisition Sustainable Growth:	Rate:
Company A: H. J. Heinz Co.	5.34%
Company B: Ore-Ida Foods, Inc.	7.72%
Post-Combination Sustainable Growth:	6.25%

Company A: Hershey Chocolate Corp.
Company B: Cory Corp.
Date of Company   1967
Method of Accounting:Purchase

Pre-Acquisition Sustainable Growth:	Rate:
Company A: Hershey Chocolate Corp.	9.85%
Company B: Cory Corp.	7.55%
Post-Combination Sustainable Growth:	16.80%

Company A: Holiday Inns
Company B: Harrah's Corporation
Date of Combination: 1980
Method of Accounting: Purchase

Pre-Acquisition Sustainable Growth: Rate:

Company A: Holiday Inns   5.90%
Company B: Harrah's Corporation   8.00%
Post-Combination Sustainable Growth: 8.40%

Company A: Kellogg Co.
Company B: Fearn International Inc.
Date of Combination: 1970
Method of Accounting: Pooling

Pre-Acquisition Sustainable Growth: Rate:

Company A: Kellogg Co.   7.67%
Company B: Fearn International, Inc.   2.03%
Post-Combination Sustainable Growth: 8.16%

Company A: Levi Strauss & Co.
Company B: Koracorp Industries, Inc.
Date of Combination: 1979
Method of Accounting: Purchase

Pre-Acquisition Sustainable Growth: Rate:

Company A: Levi Strauss & Co.   18.02%
Company B: Koracorp Industries, Inc.   28.17%
Post-Combination Sustainable Growth: 32.93%

Company A: Litton Industries, Inc.
Company B: Itek Corp.
Date of Combination: 1983
Method of Accounting: Purchase

Pre-Acquisition Sustainable Growth: Rate:

Company A: Litton Industries, Inc.   17.2%
Company B: Itek Corp.   3.4%
Post-Combination Sustainable Growth: 13.2%

Company A: Midland-Ross Corp.
Company B: National Castings Co.
Date of Combination: 1965
Method of Accounting: Pooling

Pre-Acquisition Sustainable Growth:	Rate:
Company A: Midland-Ross Corp.	5.30%
Company B: National Castings Co.	3.29%
Post-Combination Sustainable Growth:	7.65%

Company A: Monsanto Co.
Company B: Fisher Governor Co.
Date of Combination: 1969
Method of Accounting: Purchase

Pre-Acquisition Sustainable Growth:	Rate:
Company A: Monsanto Co.	5.10%
Company B: Fisher Governor Co.	6.80%
Post-Combination Sustainable Growth:	4.96%

Company A: Mosinee Paper Corp.
Company B: Sorg Paper Corp.
Date of Combination: 1983
Method of Accounting:Purchase

Pre-Acquisition Sustainable Growth:	Rate:
Company A: Mosinee Paper Corp.	5.46%
Company B: Sorg Paper Corp.	0.83%
Post-Combination Sustainable Growth:	7.47%

Company A: Philips Van Heuesen Corp.
Company B: Joseph Feiss, Inc.
Date of Combination: 1966
Method of Accounting: Pooling

Pre-Acquisition Sustainable Growth:	Rate:
Company A: Philips Van Heuesen Corp.	13.48%
Company B: Joseph Feiss, Inc.	8.26%
Post-Combination Sustainable Growth:	9.03%

Company A: Pitney Bowes Inc.
Company B: Dictaphone Corp.
Date of Combination: 1979
Method of Accounting: Purchase

Pre-Acquisition Sustainable Growth: Rate:

Company A: Pitney Bowes Inc.   7.54%
Company B: Dictaphone Corp.   3.40%
Post-Combination Sustainable Growth: 7.71%

Company A: Quaker Oats Co.
Company B: Stokley-Van Camp, Inc.
Date of Combination: 1983
Method of Accounting: Purchase

Pre-Acquisition Sustainable Growth: Rate:

Company A: Quaker Oats Co.   8.86%
Company B: Stokley-Van Camp, Inc.   8.06%
Post-Combination Sustainable Growth: 14.22%

Company A: R. J. Reynolds Tobacco Co.
Company B: Penick & Ford, Inc.
Date of Combination: 1965
Method of Accounting: Purchase

Pre-Acquisition Sustainable Growth: Rate:

Company A: R. J. Reynolds Tobacco Co.   8.58%
Company B: Penick & Ford, Inc.   3.72%
Post-Combination Sustainable Growth: 8.19%

Company A: Revlon, Inc.
Company B: U.S. Vitamin & Pharmaceutical Corp.
Date of Combination: 1966
Method of Accounting: Pooling

Pre-Acquisition Sustainable Growth: Rate:

Company A: Revlon, Inc.   10.97%
Company B: U. S. Vitamin   3.34%
Post-Combination Sustainable Growth: 8.25%

```
Company A: Smithkline Corporation
Company B: Beckman Instruments Inc.
Date of Combination:   1981
Method of Accounting: Pooling

Pre-Acquisition Sustainable Growth:               Rate:

Company A: Smithkline Corporation                 22.90%
Company B: Beckmann Instruments, Inc.             10.60%
Post-Combination Sustainable Growth:              16.80%
```

```
Company A: Susquehanna Corp.
Company B: Atlantic Research
Date of Combination:   1967
Method of Accounting: Purchase

Pre-Acquisition Sustainable Growth:               Rate:

Company A: Susquehanna Corp.                       1.50%
Company B: Atlantic Research                      13.15%
Post-Combination Sustainable Growth:              19.36%
```

```
Company A: U.S. Steel Corp.
Company B: Alside Inc.
Date of Combination:   1968
Method of Accounting: Purchase

Pre-Acquisition Sustainable Growth:               Rate:

Company A: U.S. Steel Corp.                        1.26%
Company B: Alside, Inc.                           12.14%
Post-Combination Sustainable Growth               3.81%
```

```
Company A: U.S. Steel Corp.
Company B: Marathon Oil
Date of Combination:   1982
Method of Accounting: Purchase

Pre-Acquisition Sustainable Growth:               Rate:

Company A: U.S. Steel Corp.                        7.36%
Company B: Marathon Oil                           15.00%
Post-Combination Sustainable Growth:             (7.81%)
```

Company A: Union Oil of California
Company B: The Pure Oil Co.
Date of Combination: 1965
Method of Accounting: Pooling

Pre-Acquisition Sustainable Growth: Rate:

Company A: Union Oil of California   7.28%
Company B: The Pure Oil Co.   5.46%
Post-Combination Sustainable Growth   9.25%

Company A: Ward Foods
Company B: Honolulu Iron Works
Date of Combination: 1966
Method of Accounting: Pooling

Pre-Acquisition Sustainable Growth: Rate:

Company A: Ward Foods   2.66%
Company B: Honolulu Iron Works   11.32%
Post-Combination Sustainable Growth: 18.66%

Company A: White Consolidated Industries, Inc.
Company B: Scott & Williams, Inc.
Date of Combination: 1966
Method of Accounting: Pooling

Pre-Acquisition Sustainable Growth: Rate:

Company A: White Consolidated Industries, Inc.   24.10%
Company B: Scott & Williams, Inc.   (15.50%)
Post-Combination Sustainable Growth: 35.29%

MERGERS, ACQUISITIONS, AND DIVESTITURE...
EFFECTS ON WORKERS[1]

by

John Funiciello[2]

The rush to merge, acquire, and divest is, essentially, an effort to consolidate wealth, to enhance profit-making, and to consolidate power to make further profits possible. There are many ways to view this effort to accumulate corporate wealth, but it all goes to the bottom line--making money. I'll talk briefly today about the way we do business in the United States, how our national economy has suddenly become a world economy, and how this has affected workers.

To workers, the terms buy-out, takeover, offshore production, flood of imports, and plant closings mean the same thing -- they are caught up in economic events over which they have little or no control, whether or not they work under a union contract.

As U.S. business interests enter full speed into the world economy, they are leaving behind workers whose lives are devastated and whose communities are left with tax bases which are eroded so they can't provide necessary services. We've become a service economy, and many of our manufactured goods and heavy industrial goods and materials are being imported.

Unemployment is high and underemployment is higher. The former is used to wrest concessions from those who have contracts and to intimidate those who don't have a union contract. Underemployment simply is a blot on the record of a system that prides itself on research and development and innovation in every stage of the industrial system. As well, the army of unemployed serves as a grim reminder to those who are working, that they could very well be on the street next week.

---

[1] This was a keynote address given at Siena College's Symposium on Mergers and Acquisitions

[2] Public Affairs Associate for the American Federation of State, County and Municipal Employees

Because mergers and acquisitions are a natural outgrowth of the concept of economy of scale, it seems only natural that the chief executive officers of American corporations follow the dollar. Divestiture of divisions or departments of existing companies also provide more profits for the company. Isn't that what our system is all about? People caught up in the aftermath of plant closings just have to make adjustments. People unemployed because their work has been exported will just have to retrain. Those forced into early retirement will have to find a supplemental job for the next ten years, and young people will just have to wait.

When the chemical plant decided to leave Solvay, just outside Syracuse, it left intact a plant that was capable of producing high quality soda ash. The firm bought a soda ash mine in Wyoming and, determined to eliminate competition, closed the plant. The first act upon closure was to remove the 100-foot rotating drums that dried the chemical at the end of the process. The two drums, which dated back to the turn of the century, would be hard to replace at any price. Once they were gone, the plant sat for months, with the company safe in the knowledge that nothing could be produced there without the drums.

The plant employed about 1,500 workers, about 800 of whom were union members. There were few job prospects for any of them, although there were benefits and job retraining for many.

The power generating plant that, as a separate industry, might have employed 150 workers, also was scheduled for demolition. Ironically, the soda ash from the Wyoming mine was said to contain impurities that didn't exist in Solvay. All of the buildings will be demolished to make way for a treed, grass-covered park for the shriveling community.

Why would a company do that to its workers and the community? The answer is simple. Labor costs. When it can be mined with fewer workers, why should a company manufacture it, even if it is of a much higher quality? The cost of labor is the single largest item in figuring what will cost to produce a product, excluding the cost of raw materials. To make maximum profits, a company can't skimp on raw materials, but it can chip away at the cost of labor.

Greyhound Corporation is a good example of this. In 1980, workers agreed to a concessionary contract and management promised that it would promote the charter business to make up in added work what people were losing in concessions. The company failed to keep its word during that contract and came back in 1983, asking for a total of 23 percent more in wage and benefit cuts. Eleven-thousand-five hundred workers struck the company. The status quo would have been acceptable to them, but management wanted to trim the fat, to make the intercity bus system more appealing to a potential buyer.

All the while, Greyhound chairman John Teets threatened to sell the company if the workers didn't toe the line. They eventually went back to work just before Christmas, 1983, for little more than they had when they went out on strike. In 1986, Teets, relentless, came back with more concession demands, having eliminated three thousand workers during the previous three years. Again, he threatened to sell the bus lines if they didn't accept his conditions. Again, they rejected the demands, and, although they didn't strike, Teets announced the sale of the bus lines to a Dallas company for some $350 million, leaving Greyhound with its meatpacking and food service businesses, its financial services, its consumer products business, and its bus manufacturing plants.

The new owner has said publicly that he feels no obligation to honor union contracts or any other commitments to the current workforce. Here in Albany, the Greyhound workers refused to give up contract protection, refused the company offer of a buyout of their years of service. They just wouldn't go quietly. One worker said, "It's just us and Philadelphia who're left. If we do go, we can go with our heads high." Reduced staffing has resulted in forced, continuous overtime, an exhausting and demanding way to work. The company may pay the same wage costs to a worker on overtime, as it would to a new worker, but it saves the cost of benefits by choosing to pay for overtime. Workers have dropped into lower income brackets. They supplement their Greyhound incomes. Others have found other jobs that pay less or require longer hours to make the same money.

Has the consumer benefitted? The new owner has said that deregulation of airlines and the subsequent mergers in the airline industry are likely to result in higher air fares and, therefore, people will be more willing to pay the higher fares for bus travel.

When St. Joe resources demanded concessions from
its miners in St. Lawrence county more than a year-and-
a-half ago, the miners struck the company, which
apparently felt that, with the low price of zinc, it
could try to starve the miners back to work in short
order. Even without the support of the community, the
miners and the union have held out. They eat lots of
potatoes and onions, home-grown tomatoes and pasta, and

lots of rice, but they're holding out, determined to go
back down into the mines with dignity and with fair
treatment and wages.

The price of zinc is twice the price per pound
today as it was 18 months ago. The stockholders should
know that millions of dollars are being lost while the
mines are being run by inexperienced, inefficient
strikebreakers and management personnel.

Members of the Aluminum, Brick, and Glass Workers
International Union struck Alcoa in Massena last
summer, after what has become a kind of ritual chant
for companies since the so-called Reagan revolution.
"We need to put the company in a better position," they
said to the workers, "therefore, we need concessions in
wages and benefits. Give them to us or you'll suffer
layoffs or, worse, we'll close the plant and you won't
come through the doors again."

While they were on the picket lines, Alcoa workers
heard that the company had a line ready somewhere in
Brazil. Many companies have their ace in the hole in
some other country, usually a low-wage nation where
workers have little in the way of pay and benefits, and
even less in the way of rights to organize to improve
their lives. They returned to work, but with the ever-
present threat of loss of their jobs at some time in
the future.

It was the same with the papermakers of Rumford,
Maine. Last summer, the profitable Boise-Cascade paper
mill told them it needed concessions. Workers refused,
went on strike, and paid the price. The company hired
two kinds of security firms. One was the usual, with
young men who couldn't find work anywhere else, and
older men who had no choice but to take the equivalent
of minimum wages plus expenses.

The other outfit was designed to scare the hell
out of everyone. They wore their hair in shavetail
crewcuts, combat boots, and uniforms that made them

look as if they were involved in a war game. Rumford workers told me that the community was scared as hell. A rather remote city of about 10,000, Rumford doesn't see that kind of thing much, except on television, and these guards were everywhere, at all times of the day and night, in the mill and around Rumford.

After the strike was settled, there were still 350 of the 1,200 workers outside, while strikebreakers held their jobs and bragged to returned strikers about their high pay, pay that the union had achieved over generations of collective bargaining. Rumford will never be the same.

The Clifton-Morenci area of Arizona is another that will never be the same. It's a place that is largely controlled and owned by Phelps-Dodge, the largest copper mining and smelting company in the nation. They, too, demanded concessions and the workers struck. For 32 months, they held out until it was officially lost, but not before an attack by Arizona state police and the National Guard on participants in a peaceful observance of the first anniversary of the strike. There was physical intimidation during the nearly three years, but the intimidation of knowing that their livelihoods hung in the balance was the greater. Yet, they stood firm, losing only a percentage of their strikers to the company's offers of good pay and working conditions.

It turned out as it usually does. The strike-breakers were unable to turn out the production to amount to anything. The company lost money, but continued to pay the strikebreakers, because it demoralized the strikers. Demand for copper was low, so the price was down, but the reason that prices were so low was that copper from Chile, one of the biggest suppliers in the world, was being mined under a military dictatorship which ruled the workforce with an iron fist.

During the early years of the Reagan administration, when we were told that taking care of the corporations and big business would trickle down to the people, U.S. Steel sought and received large tax breaks, and it was agreed that the money would be reinvested in physical plant, raising productivity and creating new wealth. The union backed the plan, as did both Democrats and Republicans in congress, because it made sense.

Betraying the promises made to all of them, U.S. Steel, now USX Corporation -- reflecting the change in the way they make their money -- bought Marathon Oil and left its own steel industry to die. Again the corporate managers said, "we're not in business to make steel. We're in business to make a profit."

Underlying all of this is the world economy, and the third world workers who are forced to submit to conditions that, in the past, we would not have tolerated in America. There is no relief in sight for workers who are being replaced by low-wage, off-shore production, and there is virtually no product which cannot be made more cheaply in another country.
If the cost of labor is figured into the formula of productivity and efficiency, there is no way that American workers can ever match third world labor bargains. Of the approximately 160 nations in the world the trans-national corporations have take advantage of only a dozen or so. They have dozens to go. Where does that leave American workers? It leaves them adjusting their standard of living downward.

The papers say that we have economic recovery, but the bills unpaid, the broken-down car, and the house in disrepair tell the worker there's no recovery. The president says that things are looking up and, some of them are. For example, the stock market is setting records for volume sales on a regular basis, but the single, working mother with two small children, one of them in a day care center, doesn't own any stock. She doesn't think there is a recovery and, in fact, she doesn't see too much hope for making it out of her working-poor status.

Television and movies are filled with fantasy and, especially, the way the rich live. They have endless money to spend, like the cowboys of the Saturday afternoon westerns of the 40s who never ran out of bullets. Then there's E.F. Hutton and the check-kiting schemes and the insider trading scandals. One man was said to have earned about $80 million in a short time.

But the workers are suffering. Imagine, each of you, if it were your child who faced the prospect of not getting a college education or proper medical care, just because there was not enough money. Traditionally, education has been the way out of the drudgery of manual labor or assembly line work. Now, lots of jobs are not filled with the drudgery of manual labor, but computers and high technology have brought their own special kind of drudgery. High-tech has been touted as the answer to our economic problems -- put workers behind a computer terminal, or have them make computers.

Many long-term bank employees have set up computer systems, hailed as the latest innovations for modern banking, only to find out that the new system is their replacement. This is in an industry where a pat on the back and a handshake have served for years as just reward for a job well done and for loyal and dedicated service. This, along with the insurance industry and private office work, is among the least organized occupations, so there is virtually no protection when they decide you've worked long enough.

It can always be said that the takeovers and mergers in the banking industry provided more jobs, because branch banks were springing up faster than McDonalds and Burger Kings. Maybe that's true, but look at what kind of jobs. Just above minimum wage and part-time. A saving from every angle, and every industry that can do it, does it.

Our cities are filled with people who can't find work. Our employment rate stands at about seven percent, nearly twice the rate we would have tolerated as natural unemployment thirty years ago. Minority unemployment is an indictment of a system that considers itself to have made progress in racial equality. But, age and race discrimination continue to keep good workers out of the job market. While we point to the advance of our economy, we see the average wage of workers dropping, as service jobs replace manufacturing and industrial work.

We always thought the service jobs, at least, couldn't be taken out of the country. That may be true of washing floors and emptying bed pans, but, when it comes to computers, innovative companies already have learned to move it off-shore. They only need the umbilical cord of the telephone company.

Even in the most basic of the industries of humankind, agriculture, there are ways being found to bypass small-scale domestic production and get it cheaper, either from some other country or from a conglomerate that controls or owns tens of thousands of acres of productive land.

As companies get bigger, it becomes more difficult for them to control their workforce. It no longer

73

becomes a question of, to use an antiquated term, personnel matters. It isn't even human resources management. It's just plain control of the workers. No one should be surprised at this.

With part-time employment becoming the rule, the turnover rate in our service economy -- including retailing -- is a modern phenomenon.

How to determine who is of good character? Who will be dependable? Who will be honest? Who is in good health? Whose attitudes are best for me? How can a manager determine these things quickly, at a time when the "Help Wanted" sign is framed behind glass and bolted just outside the entrance?

Simple! Give them a lie detector test when they apply. Give them another anytime anything goes wrong. Make them take a psychological test to determine how they feel about certain things, especially if he or she might vote for a union. Make them take urine tests for drugs. Maybe, even make them submit to strip searches, whenever you think it necessary. The attack on basic human and civil rights is a dangerous element of our time, because people are gradually accepting more and more of it, just for the privilege of holding a job.

Of the millions of workers who are unemployed each year, only a small percentage of them collect benefits during their unemployment. Millions more, perhaps twice the rate of the unemployed, are underemployed. These people work far below their experience, their educational level, their talent, their skill, and their creativity, and that's a loss for all of us.

Anyone who thinks unemployment rates are down should look at the rate for minorities and, especially, for teenagers. During the past six years, teenage unemployment fell from nineteen percent to 18.4 percent, but black teenage unemployment was twice or three times that rate. During the same period, the minimum wage, in 1981 dollars, fell from $3.35 per hour to $2.69, during the period when President Reagan and his advisors were strongly pushing a lower minimum wage for young people. Who could live on $6,968 a year?

With the whole world out there waiting to offer cut-rate labor prices, the corporations are hard-pressed to turn them down. One after another, American corporate heads have said publicly, "We're not human services agencies, we're in the business to make a profit." The debate over corporate social responsibility has been argued heatedly for generations and the recent catholic bishops' pastoral letter on the economy has stimulated new discussions on the issue. Like many other exclusive fraternities, corporate America would like to keep that debate in-house, making what they see as concessions only when, and as much as, they feel they are necessary.

How big is too big? How powerful is too powerful? What is the line between control and abuse? What is the business sector's responsibility to those less fortunate -- the children, the aged, the poor, the handicapped, the sick, those who've suffered discrimination, the hungry, and last -- certainly not least -- the unemployed.

We are reaching a time in history when the powerful can look right past those who are suffering at their doorstep. There's a lot of money to be made among the growing young nations. But there's a danger in ignoring such suffering and there is a danger in crushing hope for people who hoped for too long without fulfillment.

When he had witnessed the awesome power of atomic energy, Albert Einstein instantly knew what abuse of that power would mean for humanity. He said, "We shall require a substantially new manner of thinking if mankind is to survive." The gathering and wielding of awesome economic power can have similar killing effects on vast numbers of the billions of people who now inhabit the planet, if that power is not used wisely. So, I think we, also, require a substantially new manner of thinking if we are to realize the fulfillment of two of our bedrock American goals: equal opportunity for all, and a place for everyone in a society of truly free men and women, for without democracy and opportunity in our economic life, the claims of political democracy and freedom have a hollow ring.

ACQUISITION AND DIVESTITURE STRATEGY: THE STOCKHOLDERS' PERCEPTION

by

Antony Cherin and Michael Hergert[1]

ABSTRACT

A growing body of literature suggests that systematic differences in business performance can be observed between different generic strategic profiles. In this study, we extend this approach to the study of acquisitions and divestitures. An examination of the stock price performance of firms engaging in acquisitions or divestitures shows significant variation depending on the underlying business strategy of the firm.

I. INTRODUCTION

Corporate restructuring is becoming a popular tool of corporate strategy. During the first half of the 1980's, acquisition activity exceeded $100 billion per year. During the past five years, the number of divestitures increased at a similar rate, to nearly $30 billion by 1985. The focus of this study is to examine the impact on shareholder wealth from these transactions, and to analyze the role of the underlying strategy behind such business recombinations in determining stock market reaction.

Previous studies of acquisition activity have raised doubts about the effectiveness of acquisitions as a business strategy. Empirical studies by Halpern (1973), Mandelker (1974), Langetieg (1978), Dodd (1980), and Asquith (1983) in addition to earlier work surveyed in Mueller (1977), suggest that the shareholders of firms making acquisitions receive little or no financial benefit. These studies also indicate that the shareholders of acquired firms generally earn large positive returns. These findings suggest that whatever value is created in the merger process is captured by

---

[1] Respectively, Associate Professor of Finance and Associate Professor of Management, San Diego State University

the shareholders of the acquired firm. This would indicate that the appropriate strategy toward acquisition is not to purchase other firms, but to make one's company as attractive as possible to potential acquirers.

The studies mentioned above are consistent with opinions emerging in the popular press as well. A study by McKinsey & Company estimated that 28 out of 58 major acquisition programs undertaken between 1972 and 1983 failed to create returns to the acquiring firm in excess of its cost of capital. Business Week (1985) reported that one third of all acquisitions undertaken during this period were eventually undone. Skepticism about the effectiveness of acquisition strategies is growing in the boardroom. For example, Business Week (1985) reported that:

> At Fuqua Industries, Inc., where founder and Chairman J. B. Fuqua has been dismembering the conglomerate he built, the stock price has doubled since 1982. In the past, Fuqua explains, "when we made an acquisition, the stock went up. So we went out and made acquisitions." But nowadays, he notes, the rewards are generally in the other direction.

Previous research into the effectiveness of acquisition strategies typically fails to distinguish between strategic motives for making acquisitions. Asquith and Kim (1982) observed the need for such a distinction and attempted to control for synergistic versus financial effects of acquisitions by limiting their sample to conglomerate acquisitions. Their results were not significantly different from the studies which used mixed samples. Elgers and Clark (1980) made the first explicit attempt to study acquisition performance by type of acquisition strategy. They compared the stock price performance for conglomerate versus non-conglomerate acquisitions and were unable to detect a statistically significant difference between the two groups. Lubatkin (1984) in examining the relationship between merger strategies and stockholder value found that product and/or market relatedness in mergers did not necessarily result in higher values than where none existed.

The failure of these studies to demonstrate any impact of acquisition strategy on the early stock performance of acquiring firms is surprising in light of the growing body of evidence on business performance by generic strategy type. Rumelt (1974) identified eight strategic profiles ranging from single business firms to conglomerates of unrelated businesses. After relating these groups to corporate performance, he found that related-business companies were substantially more profitable than unrelated-business companies. Single business firms and companies pursuing a strategy of vertical integration were found to be somewhere in the middle. In a study of "excellent" corporations, Peters and Waterman (1982), drew a similar conclusion. They found that firms which diversify around a closely related core of skills, technologies, or customers outperformed firms which have engaged in pure conglomerate diversification. Finally, Kusewitt (1985), suggested that "industry communality" is coupled with superior performance by revealing that unrelated acquisitions are associated with greater risks to performance, as measured by ROA, on average.

At the same time, as noted by Dodd (1986), the evidence from a large body of empirical literature indicates that the wealth created in a merger transaction flows to the target firm's shareholders. The average abnormal return to bidding firms is near zero, suggesting that competition exists in the market for corporate control. This competitive environment results in profits of buying firms being bid to a level where stockholders earn normal rates of return and no more. This finding is supported by Singh (1983) and Singh and Montgomery (1984). They found that while total wealth creation in a merger is greater for related acquisitions than unrelated ones, the effects are mostly reflected in the returns to the target firm as opposed to the acquirer.

The relatively poor productivity of capital in conglomerates has led to a reduced valuation of conglomerate securities in the stock market. Both the Business Week Quarterly Survey of Profits and the Forbes Annual Industry Comparisons, as reported in Salter and Weinhold (1979), show consistent patterns of lower returns on equity and price-to-earnings ratios for conglomerate firms.

In applying these findings to the study of acquisitions, one's prior hypothesis would be that an announcement of a new acquisition would lead to a revaluation of the acquiring firm's stock price in light of the underlying strategy of the acquisition. Acquisitions which reflect a strategy of closely related diversification should be viewed more favorably than acquisitions of a conglomerate nature. Acquisitions used to achieve vertical integration should fall somewhere between the two.

A similar line of argument can be applied to divestitures. Several authors have investigated the effects of divestitures on security prices. Alexander et al. (1984) found that the announcement of a voluntary corporate selloff has a slightly positive impact on the stock returns of a firm. This is consistent with the previous work of Boudreaux (1975), Kummer (1978), Magiera & Grunewald (1978), and Miles & Rosenfeld (1983). In the case of FTC-forced divestitures, market reaction to the announcement is generally negative.

As in the case of the acquisition studies cited above, the above authors generally fail to account for any strategic motive behind the divestiture in studying the impact on shareholder wealth. Magiera and-Grunewald (1978) did make an attempt to distinguish between divestitures undertaken for change-of--business-mix motives and those due to poor financial results. They were unable to demonstrate any significant differences between these two groups.

In a more recent paper, Montgomery et al. (1984) explored the impact of divestiture strategy on stock price performance and found that divestitures which were linked to corporate or business strategies were viewed positively by the stock market. Divestitures portrayed as the sale of unwanted units were viewed negatively. They conclude that divestiture can be a useful tool of corporate strategy as long as the sale of business units can be justified as part of a cohesive strategy.

In this study, we extend the work described above to an investigation of the link between corporate strategy and acquisition/divestiture performance by examining market reaction to a sample of business recombinations categorized by underlying strategy. The six strategic alternatives discussed are: related diversification/divestiture, vertical integration/divestiture, and conglomeration/deconglomeration. The study's methodology is outlined in Section II, the sample and hypotheses are discussed in Sections III. and IV., respectively. Section V. covers the empirical results and summary comments are made in Section VI.

II. METHODOLOGY

Most of the studies described above used the technique of residual analysis to analyze the impact of acquisition or divestiture announcements. This technique is useful for isolating the abnormal returns arising from a specific event, such as the announcement of an acquisition. Residual analysis uses the market model described by Fama (1976) to estimate the normal stock market returns for a particular company. To calculate the normal returns, the following parameters of the market model are estimated:

$$r_j = \alpha_j + \beta_j r_m + e_j \qquad (1)$$

where:

r_j = return on security j

α_j = intercept term for security j

β_j = historic market relationship for security j

r_m = return on market portfolio

e_j = error term

The estimates for α_j and β_j can then be used to calculate the expected movement in an individual security price given the movement in the total market. These parameters were estimated over a 60 month period immediately preceding the announcement of an acquisition or divestiture. Equation (1) was then solved for a six week trading period centered on the announcement date. This provided the expected daily returns in the absence of extraordinary events. Abnormal returns for each firm (r^a_{jt}) were then calculated as the difference between actual and predicted returns during the six week estimation period:

$$r^a_{jt} = r_{jt} - (\alpha_j + \beta_j r_{mt}) \qquad (2)$$

In order to calculate the total effect of the announcement of an acquisition or divestiture on security prices, the abnormal returns are cumulated for the thirty one day trading period:

$$CAR_j = \sum_{t=1}^{31} r^a_{jt} \qquad (3)$$

The values of CAR_j can then be averaged across groups to compare the effect of different strategies of acquisitions and divestitures.

III. SAMPLE

The sample consisted of 109 acquisition and divestiture deals occurring during 1983, 1984, and 1985. Deals were selected on the basis of announcements appearing in the Wall Street Journal. These announcements provided two pieces of information: the date to be used as a center point for estimating abnormal returns, and the strategic rationale for the acquisition or divestiture.

Transactions were assigned to one of three strategic types: related diversification, vertical integration, or conglomeration. If the deal description did not contain sufficient information with which to assign the deal to one of these groups, the transaction was discarded as unsuitable for analysis. This procedure led to the following cell sizes for analysis:

	Related Diversification	Vertical Integration	Conglomeration
Acquisitions	29	15	18
Divestitures	18	11	18

IV. HYPOTHESES

The announcement of an acquisition or divestiture will be accompanied by a change in security prices if value is perceived as being created or destroyed by the transaction. The strategic motive for the deal should have a bearing on this process. Value can be created through operating synergy, financial effects, or risk reduction. The form and size of value creation will depend on the underlying strategic rationale of the business recombination. For example, the potential for operating synergy is relatively great for a related business acquisition or vertical integration acquisition compared to a conglomerate acquisition because the prospects for sharing costs, technologies, customers, or creating some other form of synergy is greater for businesses which are similar. To the extent that business relatedness is an explanatory factor for the productivity of capital (as argued by Rumelt and Peters & Waterman), our expected finding would be:

Abnormal Returns		Abnormal Returns		Abnormal
Related	>	Vertical	>	Returns
Diversification		Integration		Conglomerate
Acquisitions		Acquisitions		Acquisitions

The analysis of divestitures provides a check on the symmetry of the above hypotheses. If conglomerate acquisitions are viewed negatively, then the spinoff of an unrelated business unit may be viewed favorably by investors. Such a sale could signal the reversal of a firm's conglomeration strategy and produce positive abnormal returns. The prior hypotheses for divestitures which reduce the extent of vertical integration or inter-business relatedness are less clear. If relatedness is viewed positively by the market, then moves which reduce vertical integration or business inter-relatedness could lead to a reduction in stock prices. However, the evidence cited above suggests that voluntary spinoffs typically are viewed favorably by the market. Our prior hypotheses are that this response will be relatively less favorable for divestiture moves which reduce business inter-relatedness:

Abnormal Returns		Abnormal Returns		Abnormal
Related	<	Vertical	<	Returns
Diversification		Integration		Conglomerate
Divestitures		Divestitures		Divestitures

V. FINDINGS

The cumulative abnormal returns were calculated for each of the 57 firms chosen through the procedure described above. Figures 1 provides an example of the results of this analysis. For the case of Fuqua Industries, it appears that the strategy of deconglomeration was viewed favorably by the market. The cumulative residuals for Fuqua rise during the week preceding the announcement, drop briefly after the announcement date, and finish at a level substantially greater than zero.

However, the data for the entire sample of conglomerate divestitures does not conform to this pattern. As shown in Figure 2, the full sample of conglomerate divestitures shows a slight rise at the time of the announcement, but reverts to near zero by the end of the estimation period. The average cumulative residual for the entire group is -.008, or very

83

Figure 1

Cumulative Average Residuals

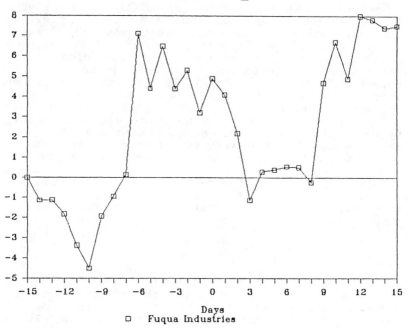

Figure 2

Cumulative Average Residuals

Divestitures

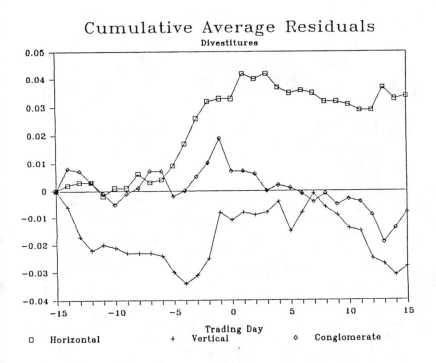

Figure 3

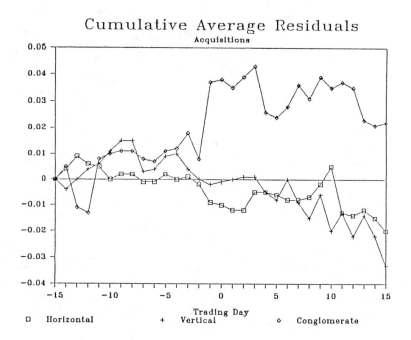

86

close to zero. Figure 2 contrasts this result to the
pattern for spinoffs which lessen the extent of
vertical or horizontal integration. These two
strategies show a much different pattern of performance. Horizontal divestitures show a sharp rise just
prior to the announcement and stabilize at about +3%.
Vertical divestitures are greeted more negatively in
the stock market. The average residual for vertical
spinoffs was -2.8%.

A similar analysis was done for each sample of
acquisition strategies. As shown in figure 3, the only
acquisition strategy to produce positive returns was
unrelated conglomeration. Surprisingly, both vertical
and horizontal acquisitions produced negative cumulative residuals. Conglomerate acquisitions show a sharp
rise in price at the time of the announcement, while
both vertical and horizontal acquisitions are relatively stable around zero throughout the estimation
interval.

In order to test the hypotheses described earlier,
pairwise t tests were run on the differences between
the mean cumulative residuals between each type of
strategy. These findings are summarized in Table 1.
The data do not support the hypotheses stated earlier.
Although the findings do not correspond to the predicted shareholder reactions, it should be noted that
very few of the end-of-period residuals were significantly different from one another. Further t test
were performed to determine if the end-of-period
residuals for each strategy were significantly-
different from zero. None of the strategies studied
produced returns which could be described as significantly positive or negative.

VI. SUMMARY AND INTERPRETATION

The results described above require careful interpretation. Contrary to the hypotheses stated earlier,
business relatedness does not seem to have a significant impact on the stock price of a firm making an
acquisition or divestiture. In light of the previous
evidence on business relatedness and corporate performance, this is a surprising result. Several underlying
phenomenon may help to explain this finding.

First, there may be difficulties in decomposing
the effect of acquisition or divestiture announcements
on security prices when the acquiring firm is substantially larger than the acquired firm. Jarrel (1983)

has suggested that when the acquired firm is relatively small, the effect of the acquisition will be difficult to detect.

A second problem in evaluating the effect of business relatedness on acquiring firm performance is the continuous nature of corporate restructuring programs. Each of the acquisitions and divestitures in this study were analyzed as discrete events. However, it may be more correct to view them as elements in a stream of decisions by firms wishing to restructure their corporate portfolios. Consequently, when an individual acquisition or divestiture is announced, it will have a far less dramatic impact on security prices. It may be more fruitful to study market reactions to the initial announcements of corporate restructuring programs, and to see if related business programs are viewed more favorably than unrelated business programs. Unfortunately "announcements" of such programs are rare, and the use of residual analysis would be problematic at best.

A third difficulty in detecting the effect of business strategy on acquisition or divestiture performance results from the use of short run stock price movements as a proxy for longer term business performance. Stock market reaction to strategic announcements should reflect the expected long run value creation (or destruction) resulting from the decision. If the market is efficient, then all available information relating to the likely long run performance of an acquisition or divestiture will be used to re-value the firm's securities in light of the new activity. One such piece of information would be the empirical observation that on average, corporations composed of related business units have a superior track record to unrelated conglomerate portfolios. Although horizontally integrated firms perform better on average, there are many significant exceptions to the rule. It may be that the market is unable to discriminate the quality of strategies during the six week trading period surrounding the announcement. The superiority of a strategy may take much longer to assess, and thus not be detectable at the time of the announcement.

A final qualification to these findings is that a study of acquiring firm stock prices may not capture the differential effects on acquired firm securities. Montgomery and Singh (1984) demonstrate that the increase in target firm stock prices may depend on the extent of business relatedness between the merger

Table 1

	Related Acquis.	Related Divest.	Vertical Acquis.	Vertical Divest.	Conglom. Acquis.	Conglom. Divest.
Related Acquis.	---					
Related Divest.	d= .054 t= 1.37	---				
Vertical Acquis.	d= .013 t= .335	d= .067 t= 2.06*	---			
Vertical Divest.	d= ..008 t= .184	d= .062 t= 1.75**	d= .005 t= .171	---		
Conglom. Acquis.	d= .042 t= 1.05	d= .012 t= .332	d= .056 t= 1.62	d= .050 t= 1.35	---	
Conglom. Divest.	d= .012 t= .273	d= .042 t= 1.01	d= .025 t= .611	d= .020 t= .436	d= .030 t= .706	---

Note:

d= difference between sample means

t= t statistic

* indicates significance at the 95% confidence level

** indicates significance at the 90% confidence level

partners. In comparing security price movements for acquiring firms, they found that relatedness did not have an appreciable effect on stock market reaction to acquisition announcements (a similar finding to the current study). However, they did find that the shareholders of the acquired firms which were similar to the bidding firm did experience a greater wealth transfer than did the shareholders for unrelated firms. Although they do not offer a compelling theory for this phenomenon, it could help to explain the results reported above.

The current boom in acquisition and divestiture activity has focused attention on the effectiveness of such strategies in creating shareholder wealth. This study has attempted to investigate the effect of type of acquisition or divestiture strategy on security performance. Our findings suggest that stock market reaction does not systematically vary with the underlying strategy of the acquisition or divestiture. returns.

This finding adds to the inventory of evidence supporting a skeptical view of proactive acquisition and divestiture strategies. Numerous studies have confirmed that shareholders of acquired firms receive a windfall of wealth from the transaction. However, these firms are passive players. The acquiring firm has greater control over its destiny. Unfortunately, there is little support for the hypothesis that the implementation of an active acquisition strategy is likely to create wealth.

References

Alexander, G.J., Benson, P.G. & Kampmeyer, J.M. Investigating the Valuation Effects of Announcements of Voluntary Corporate Selloffs. Journal of Finance, June 1984, pp.503-517.

Asquith, P. Merger Bids, Uncertainty, and Stockholder Returns. Journal of Financial Economics, November 1983, pp.51-83.

Asquith, P. & Kim, E.H. The Impact of Merger Bids on the Participating Firms' Security Holders. Journal of Finance, December 1982, pp.1209-1228.

Boudreaux, K.J. Divestiture and Share Price. Journal of Financial and Quantitative Analysis, 1975, 10, 619-626.

Do Mergers Really Work?. Business Week, June 3, 1985, pp.64-67.

Dodd, P. Merger Proposals, Management Discretion and Stockholder Wealth. Journal of Financial Economics, June 1980, pp.113-138.

Dodd, P. The Market for Corporate Control: A Review of the Evidence. Financial Management Collection, Vol. 1, No. 2, Spring 1986.

Elgers, P.T. & Clark, J.J. Merger Types and Shareholder Returns: Additional Evidence. Financial Management, Summer 1980, pp.66-72.

Fama, E.F. Foundations of Finance. New York, NY.: Basic Books, 1976.

Halpern, P. Empirical Estimates of the Amount and Distribution of Gains to Companies in Mergers. Journal of Business, October 1973, pp.554-573.

Jarrel, G. Do Acquirers Benefit from Corporate Acquisitions? Working Paper, University of Chicago, March 1983.

Kummer, D.R. Valuation Consequences of Forced Divestiture Announcements. Journal of Economics and Business, 1978, 30, 130-136.

Kusewitt, J.B. An Exploratory Study of Strategic Acquisition Factors Relating to Performance. Strategic Management Journal, 1985, pp.151-169.

Langetieg, T.C.   An Application of a Three-factor Performance Index to Measure Stockholder Gains from Merger. Journal of Financial Economics, December 1978, pp.365-384.

Lubatkin, M.   Merger Strategies and Stockholder Value. Working Paper 30-84, The University of Connecticut, December 1984.

Magiera, F.T. & Grunewald, A.E.   The Effect of Divestiture Motives on Shareholder Risk and Return.   Paper Presented at the Western Finance Association Annual Meeting, Kona, Hawaii, 1978.

Mandelker, G. Risk and Return: The Case of Merging Firms. Journal of Financial Economics, December 1974, pp.303-335.

Miles, J.A. & Rosenfeld, J.D.   The Effect of Voluntary Spin-off Announcements on Shareholder Wealth.   Journal of Finance, December 1983, pp.1597-1606.

Montgomery, C.A., Thomas, A.R. & Kamath, R.   Divestiture, Market Valuation, and Strategy.   Academy of Management Journal, December 1984, pp.830-840.

Mueller, D.C.   The Effects of Conglomerate Mergers: A Survey of the Empirical Evidence.   Journal of Banking and Finance, 1977, 1, 315-347.

Peters, J.P. & Waterman, R.H. Jr.   In Search of Excellence: Lessons from America's Best-Run Companies, New York, NY.: Harper & Row, 1982.

Rumelt, R.P.   Strategy, Structure and Economic Performance.   Boston, MA.: Division of Research, Graduate School of Business Administration, Harvard University, 1974.

Salter, M.S. & Weinhold, W.A.   Diversification Through Acquisition: Strategies for Creating Economic Value, New York, NY.: Macmillan, 1979.

Singh, H.   Corporate Acquisitions and Economic Performance.   Ph.D. Dissertation, The University of Michigan, 1983.

Singh, H. & Montgomery, C.A.   Corporate Acquisitions and Economic Performance.   Working Paper 84-13, The Wharton School, The University of Pennsylvania, 1984.

"THE CONSEQUENCES FOR STOCKHOLDERS
OF FENDING OFF UNFRIENDLY TAKEOVERS:
THE CASE OF UNOCAL VERSUS MESA PARTNERS II"[1]

by

Mark L. Gardner[2]

Introduction

Public opinion is sharply divided over whether corporate raiders such as T. Boone Pickens, Carl Icahn, and others should be permitted to take over companies which they perceive to be undervalued on the stock market. In the early 1980's there were numerous multi-billion dollar mergers - some friendly and others hostile - in the United States' petroleum industry.

A great variety of defensive tactics have been developed by managers to discourage would-be greenmailers. Among these are the "poison pill", the "golden parachute", and others too numerous to mention. The unsuccessful attempt by T.Boone Pickens to take over UNOCAL, the nation's 12th largest oil company, in 1985 will provide the springboard for a discussion of the effects of UNOCAL's defensive strategy on its stockholders. The time period covered in the paper extends from the beginning of 1984 to the end of 1986 with greatest emphasis on the period between February and October, 1985.

UNOCAL's Defensive Strategy

In February, 1985, T. Boone Pickens announced that his firm Mesa Petroleum Company--through affiliates Mesa Partners II and Mesa Eastern--had acquired 7.9 percent of UNOCAL's common stock for investment purposes only. By March, Pickens' group had acquired 13.6 percent of the shares. In April, Pickens offered to pay $54 in cash for an additional 64 million shares which would give him a controlling interest in UNOCAL. Pickens' offer was conditional on getting the required 64 million shares. The remaining shares would be purchased by issuing $54 in debt securities at a later date. (25, p. 14) (See Table 1.)

---

[1] The author acknowledges the assistance of Marvin Gardner, William O'Connor, Kevin Price & Phillip Ilnoff

[2] Chairman, Department of Business Economics, Piedmont College

TABLE 1: HIGHLIGHTS OF PICKENS' ATTEMPT TO TAKE OVER UNOCAL

Date	Event
Feb. 1985	The Pickens group announces that it has purchased 7.9 percent of UNOCAL's common stock for investment purposes.
Mar. 1985	The Pickens group has accumulated 13.6 percent of UNOCAL's stock. (23.7 million shares)
Apr. 1985	Pickens offers $54 in cash per share for 64 million UNOCAL shares which would give him 50.1 percent of the total.
	UNOCAL offers to purchase up to 49.9 percent of its stock, 87.2 million shares, for $72 each in debt securities. The Pickens group is barred from tendering its shares.
May 1985	UNOCAL extends the deadline for its offer from April 30th until May 14th.
	A Delaware court orders UNOCAL to include the Pickens group in its buyback offer. UNOCAL appeals to the Delaware Supreme Court.
	Fred Hartley, UNOCAL board chairman, and Boone Pickens begin negotiations on a possible settlement, but talks break down.
	The Delaware Supreme Court reverses the lower court's decision and allows UNOCAL to exercise its "business judgement" in excluding Pickens from the buyback.
	Hartley and Pickens resume negotiations. Pickens is allowed to tender about one-third of his 23.7 million shares in exchange for $72 worth of debt securities each. The remainder will be sold off gradually.
Aug. 1985	UNOCAL raises $141 million in case through the public sale of assets--8.6 million units of its newly formed master limited partnership, UXP. THe company retains the balance of the 211.4 million units.
Oct. 1985	UNOCAL recalls the debt securities it used to fend off Pickens at premiums of between 3 and 7 percent. These securities are refinanced at lower interest rates.

94

Fred Hartley, chairman of UNOCAL's board, responded to the possibility of an unfriendly takeover in several ways. Pickens had previously been involved in unfriendly takeover attempts at Cities Service, Gulf, and Phillips Petroleum. As early as 1983, UNOCAL had eliminated cumulative voting, which could have given minority shareholders an advantage. It also staggered the terms of the board members to prevent a dissident group from obtaining control all at once. (25, pp.1 & 14)

The Pickens' group tried unsuccessfully to postpone UNOCAL's annual meeting from April 29th until June 28th so that it could come up with a slate of candidates to oppose those proposed by management. Hartley responded by assigning 900 UNOCAL employees to work full time and by hiring outside help to win the proxy battle. (25, p. 14)

When it appeared that the Mesa group might be successful in getting effective control of UNOCAL, Hartley came up with a counter-offer for the stockholders. He offered to purchase up to 87.2 million shares in exchange for $72 worth of three different types of debt securities. This proposal would have given the UNOCAL's management control of 49 percent of the outstanding stock and saddled the company with a huge debt burden. Despite the prospect of obtaining a debt-ridden company, Pickens seemed determined to swallow this "poison pill". But an unusual move by UNOCAL prohibited the Mesa group from tendering its shares. (25, p. 14)

Pickens and his associates immediately filed suit in Delaware where UNOCAL was chartered. The state court upheld the Pickens challenge and ordered UNOCAL to include Mesa in its offer. On UNOCAL's appeal to the Delaware Supreme Court, the lower court's decision was reversed. UNOCAL was allowed to exercise its "business judgement" in excluding Mesa. This decision was not appealable to the federal courts since this issue was considered to be under the jurisdiction of the states. (10, p. 35) and (31, p. 2)

Prior to the reversal of the lower court decision Pickens and Hartley had begun to negotiate a settlement, but talks had broken down. Now that UNOCAL's exclusionary clause had been upheld, both Hartley and Pickens were anxious to settle. Pickens was allowed to sell 7.7 million of the 23.7 million shares which his group had accumulated directly to

UNOCAL in exchange for $72 each in debt securities. The remaining 16 million shares would be sold off gradually at a rate over which UNOCAL would have some control. (25, p. 14)

Of the 87.2 million shares sought unconditionally by UNOCAL, some 57.8 million were actually tendered. The company's long-term debt increased from $1,122 million at the end of 1984 to $5,520 million at the end of 1985. (See Table 2.) In order to raise cash to help pay for its higher interest costs and anti-takeover expenses of about $210 million (in 1985), UNOCAL spun off about 46 percent of its domestic oil and gas properties into a master limited partnership-- Union Exploration Partners. Approximately 8.6 million of the 211.4 million units in UXP were put on the market to raise $141 million in cash. Another 3.3 million units were distributed to stockholders as a supplemental dividend at the end of 1985. The value of the distribution at the time was about $54 million. The company retained control of approximately 95 percent of the units. (33, p. 33)

UNOCAL has consolidated and refinanced at lower interest rates most of the debt it incurred in fighting off Pickens. Its three anti-takeover debt issues were recalled at premiums ranging from 3 to 7 percent in October, 1985--less than five months after the settlement with Pickens. Despite its success in placing the debt with various lenders, UNOCAL's financial problems would appear to be far from over. (33, pp. 27 and 36)

UNOCAL and Its Competitors

UNOCAL is not the only oil company which has taken on increased debt to protect itself from a hostile takeover. Indeed, it is difficult to find a company that has not been affected by a takeover threat in some way. EXXON, the world's largest integrated oil company, was one of the few firms which was able to protect itself without either taking over another firm or being taken over, and without significantly increasing its debt burden. It has engaged in a nearly continuous program of buying back its stock. Between 1984 and 1986 EXXON succeeded in retiring over 9 percent of the total outstanding. (See Table 2.) EXXON serves as a bellwether against which the performance of other integrated companies such as UNOCAL may be judged.

TABLE 2: A COMPARISON OF UNOCAL'S AND EXXON'S
FINANCIAL PERFORMANCE, 1984-1986

Year Ending	Earnings ($ mill.)	Shares Outstanding (millions)	Earnings per Share	Long-term Debt/ Equity
		UNOCAL		
1984	$700	173.7	$4.03	.20
1985	$325	137.8	$2.36	.40
1986 est.	$145	116.0	$1.25	.17
Pct. Chg. (84-86)	(-79%)	(-33%)	(-69%)	n.a.
		EXXON		
1984	$5528	783	$6.77	.18
1985	$5415	731	$7.43	.17
1986 est.	$3700	710.0	$5.20	.24
Pct. Chg. (84-86)	(-33%)	(-9%)	(-23%)	n.a.

Note: Estimates were obtained from The Value Line Investment Survey, April 11, 1986, pp. 410 and 430, and the 1985 UNOCAL Annual Report

TABLE 3: A COMPARISON OF UNOCAL'S AND EXXON'S STOCK PRICE MOVEMENTS 1985 & 1986

1985	UNOCAL	EXXON
Jan. 1 (Jan.2)	$35.9	$44.5
Apr. 1	$49.8	$50.5
Jul. 1	$29.8	$52.6
Oct. 1	$29.0	$53.0
1985 High-Low	$55.0-26.1	$55.9-44.5

1986	UNOCAL	EXXON
Jan. 1 (Jan.2)	$27.5	$54.5
Apr. 1	$20.5	$55.5
Jul. 1	$20.1	$61.3
Oct. 1	$22.9	$67.9
1986 High-Low	$30.3-15.6	$71.3-48.4

Sources: Various issues of The Wall Street Journal.

Both UNOCAL and EXXON experienced a drop in total earnings and per share earnings despite a reduction in the number of shares outstanding. (See Table 2.) UNOCAL's 1986 earnings are expected to be at least 79 percent lower than they were in 1984 and earnings per share are expected to be at least 69 percent lower. In EXXON's case, total earnings are expected to drop by about 33 percent and earnings per share by 23 percent for the same period.

One reason for the drop in earnings was the fall in the price of crude oil, especially in the first half of 1986. UNOCAL's performance was further crippled by its heavy interest burden. As a percentage of its stockholder's equity, UNOCAL's long-term debt increased from 20 percent at the end of 1984 to 340 percent at the end of 1985. EXXON's comparable figures were 18 and 17 percent, respectively.

UNOCAL's and EXXON's stock prices reflected the underlying profitability of the companies during this period. (See Table 3.) UNOCAL's stock began 1985 at about $35 per share, briefly reached a height of $55 during the takeover effort, and closed at about $26 after the takeover effort was defeated. EXXON's stock value fluctuated in a fairly narrow range of between $55.9 and $44.5 during 1985.

As oil prices dropped in early 1986, most oil stocks also fell in value. EXXON bottomed out at $48.4, while UNOCAL dropped to slightly below $16 per share. Later in the year, interest rates continued to fall driving up the price of most stocks, including oil stocks. OPEC also seemed to reach an agreement to prevent a further erosion in oil prices. As of December 1, 1986, UNOCAL's price had recovered to equal its 1985 low of $26--about $9 or 25 percent below its pre-takeover price of $35. EXXON was trading at $69 on the same date--about $20 or 40 percent above its 1985 low of $48.4.

Concluding Remarks

It would appear that charges made by corporate raiders that management is willing to go to nearly any extreme to protect its power and privilege have some merit. The additional debt load assumed by many oil companies to fend off takeovers will undoubtedly have an adverse effect on earnings for years to come, barring some unforeseen increase in the price of oil.

Fred Hartley has been among the most vocal of oil industry executives in support of a new variable "fee" on imported oil. (9, page unknown) The fee would equal the difference between the lower price of imported oil and a presumably fixed price for domestic oil. This tariff would effectively put a price floor of $27, or $25, per barrel under the price of domestic oil. (Hartley lowered the proposed floor after the steep drop in crude oil prices in early 1986.) The bill's passage would amount to one more victory of a special interest group at the expense of the general public.

The restructuring which is continuing to occur in the petroleum industry may have some beneficial long-term effects. Peter Drucker, who is generally opposed to hostile takeovers, sees some positive results. According to Drucker, an integrated oil company has at least two types of investors--

1) those interested in a steady current income from the refining and marketing end of the business, and
2) those who want to speculate on changes in the value of the company's reserves over time. Drucker is in favor of Pickens' proposal to split up oil companies into two or more parts. UNOCAL and many others, including Mesa, have followed Pickens' advice by spinning off their oil and gas properties into master limited partnerships. (6, p. 236)

Drucker is concerned that the managers of America's largest corporations have lost their constituencies. When a raider comes along with an offer that is slightly higher than the current stock price, shareholders are likely to accept the offer. (6, p. 237) He observed that in at least one case (Phillips Petroleum) extensive stock ownership by the employees help to thwart two takeover bids. He also proposed giving management greater voting power when they are performing well than when they are not. (6, p. 246) This practice, which has already been implemented by several firms, would violate the principle of "one share, one vote" advocated by the raiders, especially Pickens.

Managers of our large petroleum companies already have more than enough power to fend off hostile takeovers. Giving them increased voting power on certain types of stock would be inviting them to change the by-laws more in their favor. Demanding that all stockholders be treated alike or that the time allowed to accept a tender offer to be extended may also work to the advantage of current management. They have primary control over the company's reserves in the form of partnership units which may be liquidated at any time to finance a takeover defense.

The corporate raiders, arbitragers, and their associates are not without their faults as is evidenced by the Boesky scandal. Current securities laws seem adequate to assure prosecution and conviction of the most blatant offenders. Despite the many roadblocks (often called "shark repellant") that have been put in the way of outside raiders, they have continued to be willing to borrow huge sums of money at high rates of interest to challenge managers whom they view as inside raiders. (12, p. 21)

Bibliography

1. Bleakley, Fred R., "Unocal Offers 28.8% Share Buyback",The New York Times, April 24, 1985, pp. D1 & D27.

2. Celarier, Michelle, "Merger-Mania Gyrates with Tax Reform": John Blair deal illustrates twists and turns in Wall Street's stance", Crain's New York Business, June 16, 1986, pp. 12 & 14.

3. Cole, Robert J. "New Tactics as UNOCAL Hits Back",The New York Times, April 30, 1985, pp. D1 & D6.

4. Davidson, Kenneth M. Mega-mergers: Corporate America's Billion-dollar Takeovers, Ballinger Publishing: Cambridge, Mass., 1985.

5. DeAngelo, Harry and Linda & Edward M. Rice, "Going Private: Minority Freezeouts and Stockholder Wealth", Journal of Law and Economics, vol. XXVII, April, 1984, pp. 367-401.

6. Drucker, Peter F., "The Hostile Takeover and Its Discontents", THe Frontiers of Management: Where Tomorrow's Decisions Are Being Shaped Today, E.P. Dutton: New York, 1986, pp. 231-256.

7. Fisher, Harvey, "Kean Backs Anti-Takeover Bill", Crane's New York Business, June 23, 1986, p.2.

8. Geewax, Marilyn, "Fed Action Won't Clean Out All 'Junk'", The Atlanta Journal and Constitution, Dec. 16, 1985, p. 4-E.

9. Hartley, Fred L. "Why Cheap Oil Is No Boon for the U.S.: A Peril To Security", The New York Times, March 30, 1986, reprint, page unknown.

10. Hayes, Thomas, "UNOCAL Bar to Pickens is Upheld" The New York TImes, May 18, 1985, p. 35 and 45.

11. Haitani, Kanji, Comparative Economic Systems: Organizational and Managerial Perspectives, Prentice-Hall: Englewood, Cliffs, N.J., 1986.

12. Iseman, Frederick, "Let Corporate Takeovers Keep Rolling", The New York Times, Dec. 1, 1986, p. 21.

13. James, Christopher, "An Analysis of the Effects of State Acquisition Laws on Managerial Efficiency: The Case of the Bank Holding Company Acquisitions", _Journal of Law and Economics_, vol.XXVII, April, 1984, pp. 211-226.

14. Koepp S., "A Shark Loses Some of Its Teeth [T.B. Pickens loses battle for Unocal]", _Time_, 125:58, Je 3, 1985.

15. Manne, Henry G., "The Real Boesky-Case Issue", _The New York Times_, Nov. 25, 1986, p. 27.

16. Manne, Henry G. (ed.), _Economic Policy and the Regulation of Corporate Securities_, American Enterprise Institute: Washington, D. C. , 1969.

17. Manne, Henry G., "Controlling the Giant Corporation: Myths and Realities", in _Corporate Governance: Past and Future_, edited by Henry G. Manne, K. C. G. Productions, Inc.: New York, N. Y., 1982, pp. 125-139.

18. Meadows, Laura, "The Master At Work", _Forbes_, Oct.7, 1985, p. 100.

19. Norman, J.R., "Does Boone Pickens Practice What He Preaches" [Produced the lowest profits and shareholder gains for his pay] _Business Week_, May 6, 1985, p. 82.

20. Parisi, A.J., "Will Mergers and Buybacks Mean Less Oil Later" _Business Week_, May 20, 1985, pp. 62.

21. Pauley, David, "Merger Ethics Anyone?", _Newsweek_, Dec. 9, 1985, pp. 48-49.

22. "Pickens offers $2 billion for energy firm", _The Atlanta Constitution_, Dec. 4, 1986, pp.1-B & 8-B.

23. Potts, Mark. "After Boesky and the Goodyear Bid, New Clamor for Restraints", _The Washington Post National Weekly Edition_, Dec., 8, 1986, pp. 19-20.

24. Prokesh, Steven. "Executives Favor Curbs on 'Raiders'", _The New York Times_, Nov. 24, 1986, pp. 19 & 24.

25. Rose, Fredrick, Laurie P. Cohen, and James B. Stewart, "Battle of Titans--How T. Boone Pickens Finally Met His Match: UNOCAL's Fred Hartley", _The Wall Street Journal_, May 24, 1985, pp. 1 & 4.

26. Rotbart, Dean. "Delaware Court Ruling Might Have Changed the Way Hostile Takeovers Game Is Played", The Wall Street Journal, May 22, 1985, p. 63.

27. Samuelson, Robert J. "In Praise of Boone", Newsweek, May 6, 1985, p. 59.

28. Shepard, William G. Public Policy Toward Business, 7th ed., Richard D. Irwin: Homewood, IL, 1985.

29. Silk, Leonard, "The Peril Behind the Takeover Boom", The New York TImes, Dec. 29, 1985, p. F1 & F6.

30. Smith A. "Mergers and Impositions", Esquire, 104, Sept., 1985, p. 75-76.

31. Stewart, James B. and Laurie P. Cohen, "UNOCAL Truce Poses Possibility That Golden Era for Raiders is Waning", The Wall Street Journal, May 22, 1985, pp. 2.

32. "T. Boone Pyrrhus" [raid on UNOCAL], Forbes, 136, Aug. 12, 1985, pp. 34-35.

33. UNOCAL, Annual Report to Stockholders, 1984, Los Angeles.

34. UNOCAL, Annual Report to Stockholders, 1985, Los Angeles.

35. Value Line Investment Survey, April 3, 1986, pp. 410 & 430.

36. "Wasteful Games of America's Corporate Raiders", The Economist, vol. 295, June 1, 1985, pp. 73-76.

37. Williams, Winston, "Corporate America Buys Itself Back", The New York Times, Aug. 17, 1986, pp. 1, 6, & 7F.

38. Willoughby, J., "Greenmail Sharing", Forbes, vol. 135, April 22, 1985, pp. 38-39.

THE IMPACT OF MERGERS AND ACQUISITIONS ON RESEARCH AND DEVELOPMENT EXPENDITURES[1]

by

Dr. Thomas J. Kopp and Mr. Paul Ruggeri[2]

Introduction

Mergers and Acquisitions are not only big business, they are big news. Hostile takeovers, white knights and poison pills fill the pages of financial journals and our television news broadcasts. More importantly, mergers and acquisitions have entered the forefront of the corporate decision maker's consciousness. CEO's are putting their firms through mergers, spinoffs, selloffs, and buybacks in order to keep their shareholders happy, maintaining their firm's independence. In doing so, they have initiated the greatest reshuffling of corporate assets in American history.

The effect of this activity has been a schizophrenic approach to wealth/profit maximization. While seeking those acquisitions which provide a bargain way to raise share values, firms have also focused sharp attention on quarterly profit and dividend numbers, with an eye toward keeping their shareholders' loyalty. This short-run mentality may have serious long-run implications. Some activities whose investment returns occur over an extended time horizon or whose returns are uncertain may receive less than adequate attention. One such investment may be the firm's Research and Development.

Investment in science has long been given prominence in economic literature as a crucial factor in any nation's long-term economic growth. Joseph Schumpeter spoke of this technical progress as the driving force in the success of modern capitalism[3]. It

[1] This research was supported by a grant from Siena College

[2] The authors are Assistant Professors of Finance at Siena College

[3] Schumpeter, Joseph. Can Capitalism Survive, Harper Row 1978

has long been assumed that such progress is essential for an economy to realize productivity gains.

Recent studies have focused on those factors which determine a firm's total level of expenditure on R&D. The work by such pioneers as Edwin Mansfield and Fred Scherer along with newer research such as that by Albert Link, have suggested the following factors as key in explaining these expenditures:[4]

1. Firm Size (only among smallest firms)
2. Profits
3. Product Diversification
4. Manager versus Owner Control
5. Amount of Federal R&D Funding
6. Market Power

These studies have done little to examine the role that mergers and acquisitions may play in explaining observed changes in R&D spending. Therefore we choose to examine the effect mergers and acquisitions have on the levels of such investment in the post-combination firm. This approach diverges from the traditional focus upon R&D determinants, because we believed such a procedure would mask the issues we wish to examine. For these reasons, we began by examining the change in R&D which occurred after Mergers and Acquisitions.

However, this approach also manifests some of the problems inherent within the traditional "determinants of R&D" approach. Every year, the firm alters its level of R&D, usually keeping a target level associated with a percent of sales and adjusting this for changes in economic as well as internal factors. Therefore, the factors which determine R&D are the chief determinants in this adjustment process.

To avoid this, we focus upon the unexpected changes in R&D. Holding everything else constant, the combination of two firms should lead to an R&D expenditure level at least as large as the sum of the prior R&D levels of the individual firm. Any deviation from this must be explained by changes which occur between these two points in time. Therefore, we address the question, "Can we identify some of the factors which cause newly combined firms to adjust the level of R&D spending?"

---

[4] Link, Albert. <u>Research and Development in U.S. Manufacturing</u>, Praeger 1981

The Data Set

The data was collected using the 1981 through 1985 Business Week Research and Development Scoreboard. We collected the subset of firms which disappeared from the Scoreboard and were acquired by other firms on the Scoreboard. This provided us with the pre and post merger data on a set of forty firms. The acquiring firm was identified using the Journal of Mergers and Acquisitions.

The Variables

PUNCHR&D, the dependent variable, is the percentage unexpected change in R&D. We defined it as R&D post combination minus the sum of the precombination R&D of the individual firms, all divided by the premerger R&D. A large component of this variable should be those changes in R&D caused not by underlying firm policy, but by the changes which occurred between the two observations. It is expressed in percentage terms since the size of the changes in R&D should be related to the initial degree of R&D intensity.

TYPE, is a zero-one dummy variable used to identify whether the merger was across the business week industry classification(0), or within the same industry classification(1). A zero may indicate either a conglomerate or vertical merger; a one usually indicates a horizontal merger. While it is unclear what sign we should expect on the estimated coefficient, Schumpeter argues that monopoly power is essential to acquire the funds necessary promote innovation. If this hypothesis is correct, we would expect the coefficient on TYPE to be positive.

PCHPCPR, the percentage change in post combination profits controls for the changes which effect the availability of funds for R&D but arise from activity not captured in our data. Such activities would include spinoffs and divestments. While the work of Link and Mansfield indicates that firm size, after some initial level is a poor predictor of R&D expenditure, it is possible that changes in size resulting from combination activity might be a significant factor in the firm rethinking its R&D commitment.

While this may seem to indicate that sales may be the appropriate measurement variable, changes in sales effect R&D only through an impact on profit. This variable may also pick up some of the impact of the business cycle (see below). We define PCHPCPR as post-

107

combination profits minus the sum of the precombination profits of the individual firms, all divided by the sum of the two firms' precombination profit. If we are correct in assuming that R&D expenditure is positively related to the availability of internal funds to finance it, the sign of the estimated coefficient should be positive.

CHPRM, the change in profit margin i calculated as the post-combination profit margin of the acquiring firm minus its pre-combination profit margin. This variable is included to control for the impact of non-size decisions which the firm can make with will effect the availability of funds for R&D. It may be that higher profit margins provide a greater dollar per unit sales available for R&D. It is also possible, however, that higher margins are achieved through sacrificing long run returns from R&D for the short run savings which R&D cuts might provide.

Other variables to control for economic conditions proved meaningless, perhaps because our sample coincides with the 81-85 recovery. We were unable to develop specific indicators for the outlook of each industry which might explain some of the unexpected variation in R&D.

The Results

Below is the regression form of the equation which provided the best fit, and a summary table of results:

$$PUNCHR\&D = b_0 + b_1\ TYPE + b_2\ PCHPCPR + b_3\ CHPRM$$

Dependent Variable -- PUNCHR&D

		Coefficient	Std. Err.	T-Value
CONSTANT	b_0	-7.61973E-02	4.615345E-02	-1.650943
TYPE	b_1	- .1062339	8.072643E-02	-1.315974
PCHPCPR	b_2	7.352072E-02	3.935037E-02	1.868362
CHPRM	b_3	-1.381216E-02	8.881938E-03	-1.555259

$F = 1.736288$ R-squared = .1264015

All of the coefficients proved significant at the 80% level of confidence.

Interpretation

In examining the results generated by applying the model to our mixed cross-section/time-series data set, we believe that several interesting relationships are revealed.

1. Type - our dummy variable for the nature of the mergers has a negative coefficient. This implies that horizontal mergers result in larger than expected decreases in post merger R&D. This could be the result of scale economies in research plus the elimination of duplicate effort. However, this requires the assumption that returns to R&D are on the margin sufficiently lower so that additional R&D is not pursued. Since the coefficient on the constant term is also negative, we know that the effect of horizontal or conglomerate mergers on R&D expenditures is likely negative as well, but certainly is not sufficiently positive to offset other negative pressures subsumed in the constant term.

2. Two complementary measures are used to isolate the impact of profit changes on the level of the firm's R&D spending. The percentage change in profits gave us the expected positive sign. This indicates that a large pool of available capital is in part shared with research, supporting prior theoretical arguments concerning the nature of R&D funding as an internal activity. It also sheds some interesting light on the prior research done concerning the relationship of size and R&D expenditure. While these changes in profits may result from a combination of divestments and acquisitions, changes in the firm's composition may be key in explaining decisions regarding R&D budgets. We believe that this variable is able to capture these effects because of the inclusion of the change in profit margins.

Profit margin identifies the funds available per unit sales. Thus while divestment or acquisition effects the pool of funds available, it also impacts the efficiency with which such funds are generated. Faced with changes in this "efficiency" the firm will alter its R&D decisions. The negative sign we obtain for this variable (CHPRM) may be attributed to competitive pressures. Firms which are experiencing declining profit margins will feel some pressure to increase expenditures on research. Such expenditures, they hope, will produce cost saving, process, or product improvements. The estimated coefficients suggest that the firms views these as necessary to turn the profit situation around.

What about the successful firm? Our results indicate that a firm demonstrating increasing profit margins will show some reduction in R&D expenditures. These results are like the chicken and the egg effect. Do decreasing investment in R&D increase margins in the short-run, or did an increasing margin reduce the perceived need for the current R&D intensity?

We find it interesting that these two variables both have to be included to explain changes in R&D. A model with only one of these fails to predict. Therefore, it seems to indicate that liquid money provides opportunity while margins provide incentive. Profits will be spent. Whether they are spent on slow return activities such as R&D will be a function of the current profit margins experienced by the firm. Declining profit margins appear to make the firm more introspective.

3. In addition to the final model presented here, there are other variables we feel might contribute to the explanation of unexpected changes in post-combination R&D expenditures. Measures designed to reflect general economic outlook, such as changes in GNP, and changes in overall capacity utilization rates, failed to demonstrate any significance. We also examined changes in industry spending on R&D in the hopes of capturing a change in the firm's decision as a response to competition. These failures are likely related to the time period under consideration, the 81-85 recovery, and the composition of the sample.

Implications

The results provide some general insights into the determinants of changes in R&D expenditure. While we feel that further research on these relationships may alter the size of the coefficients, each of our attempts supports our conclusions concerning the signs. Thus this research in our opinion allows us to make some inferences:

1. Combination activity generally leads to a decline in R&D expenditure. Sixty-five percent of the unexpected post-combination changes in R&D are negative. In addition, the estimated constant term was negative for all runs.

2. Horizontal mergers, in addition to their impact on concentration, also have negative implications for total R&D expenditures. Thus applications for merger based on exploitation of technology possessed by the acquired firm should be carefully examined by regulatory authorities.

3. A necessary condition for combination to lead to increased R&D expenditure is that the post-combination firm is more profitable. However, this condition is not sufficient. Perhaps the Pickens, Ichan claim that their activity increases society's welfare is valid. What we can be sure of is that combination causes a firm to alter its immediate focus on R&D in some consistent ways. If R&D is an important component of future national economic strength, then this change in behavior may have important implications.

CAUSAL FACTORS IN U.S. MERGER MOVEMENTS[1]

by

John J. Clark, Alok K. Chakrabarti,
Thomas C. Chiang, and Gerard T. Olson[2]

INTRODUCTION

The search for causation underlying merger activity generally follows two paths. One route examines the decisions of management, shareholders, and other interested parties as to the merger of companies they control and whose performance affects their economic well being. Steiner, for example, identified thirteen motives to explain particular combinations [28]. The thought here is that an understanding of particular mergers will also contribute to an understanding of trends and waves in aggregate merger activity. The second route seeks to identify macro-economic variables which create a <u>climate</u> conducive to merger activity. Stigler [29], examines merger waves for the turn of the century to 1950, and concluded that the expansion of the capital markets was a major reason for the initial growth in merger waves. Nelson [20] focused on two variables: stock prices as the indicator of the level of activity in the capital market and the index of Industrial Production to measure industrial activity in the economy. Nelson observed that stock prices closely correlated with

[1]   This is a revised version of a paper presented at the Eastern Finance Association meeting in April 1985. We would like to thank Professor Muler-Groeling for constructive comments and research support form Drexel University. This work has been partially supported by a grant from the Division of Industrial Science and Technological Innovation at the National Science Foundation. Grant No. 83-10116.

[2] Respectively Royal H. Gibson, Sr. Professor of Business Administration at Drexel University, Mackie Professor of Commerce of Engineering at Drexel University, Associate Professor of Finance at Drexel University, and Assistant Professor of Finance at Villanova University

113

merger activity in periods of expansion while the index of Industrial Production was a better indicator of merger activity in contraction. More recently, the relationship between merger activity and capital markets was further investigated by Mandelker [15] and Chappell and Cheng [4]. They found that Tobin's "q", defined as the ratio of market value of capital goods and reproduction costs, is a signal for direct investment or indirect investment by combination. This paper takes the second path and examines the interrelationships between merger activity and particular macro-economic variables.

While Nelson's results are of considerable interest, he left many questions unanswered. His analysis did not evaluate the nature of the specific relationships between the variables, i.e., whether or not it was contemporaneous. Also, the correlational analysis used by Nelson was an insufficient measure of causality. He did not incorporate the information embodied in the time series to predict merger movements. In this paper we present empirical evidence on these questions and have constructed time series models from which causal relationships between merger activity, stock prices, and industrial production can be investigated. On the basis of the information derived from the causality tests, we are able to formulate a merger equation pertinent to the predictive purpose.

The organization of the paper is as follows. Section II deals with time series models pertinent to causality tests, including Granger's direct test and Sims two-sided regression test. Section III reports the regression results and the F statistics for the causality test. Section IV discusses the empirical implications of causality tests and formulates an optimal equation for the projection of merger activity. Section V contains the summary conclusions.

METHODOLOGY

The methodology of the causality test was originally proposed by Granger [8] and later elaborated by Sims [26], Haugh [9], Pierce and Haugh [21], Schwert [24], Khan [12], and Mehra and Chiang [17]. Granger defines causality as a reduction in forecasting variance with respect to a particular information set [30]. Specifically, if X and Y represent two time series sets and if past information about X can be used to obtain a more accurate forecast of the predicted value of Y than can be obtained from past information about Y alone, then Y can be said to be caused by X. This may be expressed as:

$$V^2_{yx} [Y_t|Y_{t-s},X_{t-s}] < V^2_y [Y_t|Y_{t-s}], \quad s \geq 1,$$

where V^2_{yx} denotes the variance of errors in forecasting Y_t based on the past information of Y_{t-s} and X_{t-s}; V^2_y denotes the variance of errors in forecasting Y_t given past values of Y_{t-s} alone. Since V^2_{yx} is smaller than V^2_y, Y is said to be caused by X in the Granger sense.

The Granger Test

Based on the notion of improving predictability, we first constructed the Granger direct test [8]. The Granger procedure of a bivariate representation involves estimating the regression, which can be specified as:

$$\blacktriangle Y(t) = \Sigma \; a(k) \; \blacktriangle Y(t-k) + \Sigma \; b(j) \blacktriangle X(t-j) + e(t) \qquad (1)$$

where $\blacktriangle Y(t)$ and $\blacktriangle X(t)$ are two stationary series and $a(k)$ and $b(j)$ are, respectively, the corresponding coefficients, $e(t)$ is a disturbance term without serial correlation. Under the null hypothesis that $\blacktriangle X(t)$ does not cause $\blacktriangle Y(t)$, the procedure involved is to test if $b(j) = 0$ for $j = 1,2,...n$. This can be done by calculating the F statistic. If the null hypothesis is rejected, it can be inferred that the $\blacktriangle X$ causes $\blacktriangle Y$. Performing the test in the reverse direction by placing $\blacktriangle X$ as the dependent variable allows us to test the hypothesis that $\blacktriangle Y$ does not cause $\blacktriangle X$. The procedure is given below:

$$\blacktriangle X(t) = \Sigma \; a(k) \; \blacktriangle X(t-k) + \Sigma \; b(j) \blacktriangle Y(t-j) + e(t) \qquad (2)$$

The hypothesis to be tested is that $B(j) = 0$ for $j = 1,2,...n$. The rejection of the hypothesis implies that $\blacktriangle Y$ causes $\blacktriangle X$. It should be noted that, in light of equations (1) and (2), the contemporaneous term may be included in the system to test the hypothesis that no causation exists "at all". That is, it involves the testing for the restrictions $b(j) = 0$ and $B(j) = 0$ for $j = 0,1...n$.

The Sims Test

The Sims test [26] of the hypothesis that $\blacktriangle Y$ does not cause $\blacktriangle X$ involves testing whether the coefficients on the future values are significant in two-side lag regression.

$$\blacktriangle Y(t) = \Sigma\ a(j)\ \blacktriangle X(t-j) + \Sigma\ b(j)\blacktriangle X(t+j) + e(t) \qquad (4)$$

where A(j) is the coefficient on the current and lagged values of $\blacktriangle X$ and B(j) is the coefficient on the future values of $\blacktriangle X$. To test the hypothesis that $\blacktriangle Y$ does not cause $\blacktriangle X$, involves testing if B(j) = 0. If the null hypothesis is rejected it can be concluded that $\blacktriangle Y$ causes $\blacktriangle X$.

Likewise, the reverse causation can be tested by fitting the following regression.

$$\blacktriangle X(t) = \Sigma\ a(j)\ \blacktriangle Y(t-j) + \Sigma\ b(j)\blacktriangle Y(t+j) + e(t) \qquad (4)$$

Once again, the null hypothesis to be tested is b(j) = 0 for j = 1,2...n. Rejection of this null hypothesis would suggest that $\blacktriangle X$ causes $\blacktriangle Y$.

On the basis of equations (3) and (4), four possible outcomes may be considered as given by Khan [12]:

(i)   If both B(j) - 0 and b(j) = 0 are rejected, then two-way causality of the two variables is concluded.
(ii)   If both B(j) = 0 and b(j) = 0 are not rejected, then a possible contemporaneous relationship is indicated.
(iii) If B(j) = 0 is rejected and b(j) = 0 is not rejected, a unidirectional causality running from $\blacktriangle Y$ to $\blacktriangle X$ is concluded.
(iv)   If B(j) = 0 is not rejected and b(j) = 0 is rejected, a unidirectional causality running from $\blacktriangle X$ to $\blacktriangle Y$ is indicated.

Before we conclude this section and proceed to conduct empirical tests, the warning provided by Zellner [30] should be pointed out. He noted that the "causality" based on statistical significance does not necessarily imply the economic causation. Rather, the attribution of causation should be derived from a given economic theory (or law) that accurately reflects the underlying economic structure. Clearly, the present study is not a case of "measurement without theory." Our empirical work is based on an observed economic phenomenon previously elaborated by several researchers [4,5,19,10,28] and one of our purposes is to examine the empirical validity of their studies.

Empirical Results

To test the hypothesis about the relationship between merger activity, stock prices, and industrial production, we used the following sets of data. The merger data was obtained from the Federal Trade Commission's annual data on mergers in mining and manufacturing with assets of $1 million or more for 1919-79. Industrial production was measured by the index of Industrial Production and stock prices by the Standard and Poor's Stock Price Index covering the same time period. The justification for using annual data is that it allows us to compare the model and the empirical results with the existing work by Nelson [20], Shughart and Tollison [25], and others [5].

In terms of equations (1) through (4), denotes the number of mergers; X applies to the stock prices (S); and to industrial production (Q). A notation stands for the first difference operator. Since the data are expressed by current prices, it is likely that the series are positively correlated over time. In order to remove this spurious correlation due to trend factors, each variable was transformed by taking the first difference on the original data. To estimate the regression models as those specified as (1) to (4), one has to truncate the length of the lag distribution of the series under study. Accordingly, all the equations were restrained to fourth orders on lagged and future variables (m = n = 4) in the estimation.[3] The decision was based on the experiments that the omitted tails of the lag distributions contribute negligible explanatory power [26]. Our experimental results were found very close to the optimal lag derived from the minimum of Final Prediction Error [11].

To implement empirical tests, equations (1) through (4) were estimated twice for the variables of interest, once with the restriction that the b(j) or B(j) equal zero and once without that constraint. The former is usually called the restricted equation and the latter the unrestricted equation. These specifications allow us to assess the explanatory power

---

[3] It is acknowledged that time series models depicted by equations (1) through (4) are quite sensitive to the included and excluded variables. For instance, using equation (1) as an example, if the lag length of ▲Y(t-k) is under-estimated, this might cause an error that would lead to rejecting null hypothesis b(j) = 0. Likewise, if the order of ▲X(t-j) is under-estimated, an error may result in that the null hypothesis, b(j) = 0, may not be rejected. On the other hand, the inclusion of too many lagged values in the equation increases the standard error of the estimates and reduces the power of the tests.

Table 1 Estimates of Granger Test Regressions for Merger Activity,
Stock Prices, and Industrial Production

No. of Equa.	Dep. Var.	Indep. Var.	Coefficient of Lagged Dependent Variable				Coefficient of Incremental Variable					R^2	F	D.W.
			a(1)	a(2)	a(3)	a(4)	b(0)	b(1)	b(2)	b(3)	b(4)			
(5)	ΔY(t)	ΔY(t-k)	0.649*	-0.669*	0.332*	-0.194						0.35	7.17	2.01
			(4.75)	(-4.26)	(2.16)	(-1.48)								
(6)	ΔY(t)	ΔY(t-k)	0.601*	-0.647*	0.285	-0.329*	1.401	2.106	0.106	0.652	12.176*	0.42	4.27	1.89
		ΔS(t-j)	(3.64)	(-3.45)	(1.53)	(-2.08)	(0.24)	(0.38)	(0.12)	(2.17)				
(7)	ΔY(t)	ΔY(t-k)	0.517*	-0.488*	0.147	-0.400*	20.716*	2.441	5.076	2.780	6.680	0.62	8.45	1.90
		ΔS(t-j)	(3.82)	(-3.12)	(0.95)	(-3.08)	(4.97)	(0.52)	(1.12)	(0.63)	(1.42)			
(8)	ΔY(t)	ΔY(t-k)	0.649*	-0.613*	0.198	-0.109*		-1.832	2.950	4.888	-3.101	0.40	3.95	1.99
		ΔQ(t-j)	(4.30)	(-3.66)	(1.12)	(-0.75)		(-0.48)	(0.77)	(1.33)	(-0.80)			
(9)	ΔY(t)	ΔY(t-k)	0.621*	-0.572*	-1.90	-0.112	2.490	-2.246	2.950	5.031	-2.950	0.41	3.52	1.99
		ΔQ(t-j)	(4.10)	(-3.19)	(1.07)	(-0.76)	(0.66)	(-0.58)	(0.76)	(1.36)	(-0.75)			

			A(1)	A(2)	A(3)	A(4)	B(0)	B(1)	B(2)	B(3)	B(4)			
(10)	ΔS(t)	ΔS(t-k)	0.036	-0.274*	-0.045*	0.397						0.30	5.43	1.90
			(0.28)	(-2.11)	(-0.34)	(2.90)								
(11)	ΔS(t)	ΔS(t-k)	-0.050	-0.143	-0.103	0.265**	0.004	-0.008		0.003		0.37	3.39	1.91
		ΔY(t-j)	(-0.30)	(-0.91)	(-0.67)	(1.66)	(0.86)	(-1.44)	(1.26)	(0.77)				
(12)	ΔS(t)	ΔS(t-k)	-0.074	-0.179	-0.114	0.060	0.017*	-0.006	0.003	0.002	0.009	0.59	7.27	1.92
		ΔY(t-j)	(-0.55)	(-1.40)	(-0.91)	(0.44)	(4.97)	(-1.40)	(0.66)	(0.42)	(0.34)			
(13)	ΔQ(t)	ΔQ(t-k)	0.170	-0.146	-0.004	-0.007						0.04	0.57	1.92
			(1.20)	(-1.01)	(-0.03)	(-0.05)								
(14)	ΔQ(t)	ΔQ(t-k)	0.167	0.001	-0.050	-0.060	0.11*	-0.016*	0.003	0.001		0.22	1.65	1.96
		ΔY(t-j)	(1.12)	(0.01)	(-0.35)	(-0.40)	(2.04)	(-2.52)	(0.46)	(0.24)				
(9)	ΔQ(t)	ΔQ(t-k)	0.173	-0.011	-0.069	-0.049	0.004	0.009	-0.004**	0.002	0.002	0.23	1.501	1.96
		ΔY(t-j)	(1.16)	(-0.07)	(-0.47)	(-0.32)	(0.66)	(1.33)	(-1.90)	(0.35)	(0.31)			

Notes:

a. ΔY= changes in merger activity; ΔX applies to ΔS, changes in stock prices, and ΔQ, changes in industrial production. Estimated equations (5) to (9) correspond to the specification of equation (1), and equations (10) to (15) correspond to (2).

b. The figures in the parentheses are statistics. D.W. denotes Durbin-Waston Statistic.

c. An asterisk (*) and double asterisks (**) indicate significance at the 5% and 10% levels, respectively.

Table 2 Estimates of Sim's Test Regressions for Merger Activity,
Stock Prices and Industrial Production

No. of Equa.	Dep. Var.	Indep. Var.	Coefficient of Future Variable				Coefficient of Current and Lagged Variable					R^2	F	D.W.
			B(4)	B(3)	B(2)	B(1)	A(0)	A(1)	A(2)	A(3)	A(4)			
(16)	ΔY(t)	ΔS(t-j)					19.929*	10.042*	-1.053	4.020	2.695	0.43	3.49	1.13
							(3.59)	(2.05)	(-0.33)	(0.68)	(0.40)			
(17)	ΔY(t)	ΔS(t+j)	8.521	5.880	-1.731	-0.241	17.753*	6.306	0.533	4.448	-1.369	0.43	3.49	1.13
		S(t-j)	(1.60)	(1.12)	(-0.31)	(-0.04)	(2.90)	(1.12)	(0.80)	(0.64)	(-0.20)			
(18)	ΔY(t)	ΔQ(t-j)					10.413*	-1.928	0.962	8.827**	-1.657	0.16	1.71	1.27
							(2.35)	(-0.40)	(0.20)	(0.68)	(0.40)			
(19)	ΔY(t)	ΔQ(t+j)	2.256	-5.591	-8.534*	4.598	7.434**	-0.664	1.341	7.497	-0.323	0.43	3.49	1.13
		ΔQ(t-j)	(0.57)	(-1.39)	(-2.09)	(1.13)	(1.71)	(-0.14)	(0.29)	(1.59)	(-0.07)			

No. of Equa.	Dep. Var.	Indep. Var.	b(4)	b(3)	b(2)	b(1)	a(0)	a(1)	a(2)	a(3)	a(4)	R^2	F	D.W.
(20)	ΔS(t)	ΔY(t-j)					0.017*	-0.006	0.001	0.002	0.011*	0.58	12.57	2.10
							(5.45)	(-1.59)	(0.19)	(0.63)	(3.55)			
(21)	ΔS(t)	ΔY(t+j)	-0.007	-0.001	0.004	-0.001	0.0018*	-0.005	0.001	0.004	0.010*	0.64	6.30	1.89
		ΔY(t-j)	(-0.29)	(0.19)	(0.95)	(-0.31)	(4.20)	(1.167)	(0.35)	(1.07)	(3.47)			
(22)	ΔQ(t)	ΔY(t-j)					0.003	0.010	(-0.012)**	-0.001	0.003	0.21	2.51	2.42
							(0.54)	(1.62)	(-1.68)	(-0.02)	(0.63)			
(23)	ΔQ(t)	ΔY(t+j)	-0.006	0.012**	-0.003	0.003	0.003	0.009	-0.0010	-0.001	0.005	0.29	1.89	1.45
		ΔY(t-j)	(-1.09)	(1.82)	(-0.45)	(0.42)	(0.45)	(1.23)	(-1.42)	(-0.004)	(1.03)			

Notes: See Table 1.

of incremental variables in the Granger and the Sims tests by conducting F test. The regression results pertinent to the Granger test are presented in Table 1, while Table 2 reports the results using Sims technique. In general, the two procedures yield similar results.

Let us first examine the relationship between the change in merger activity ($\triangle Y$) and the change in stock prices ($\triangle S$). The evidence in Table 1 indicates that the lagged value of $\triangle S$ appears to be statistically significant. However, when the contemporaneous term is taken into account, the estimated coefficient on the contemporaneous term becomes more significant as reflected in a higher t ratio and a higher R^2 value (see equation (7) in Table 1).[4] The reverse causal relationship was also examined. The result also shows that the contemporaneous coefficient is highly significant (see equation (12)). The combined evidence suggests that $\triangle S$ and $\triangle Y$ are correlated contemporaneously.[5] As we turn to the Sims regression in Table 2, a similar conclusion is reached. This is displayed in high significance on the contemporaneous coefficients and statistical insignificance on the future values (see equations (17) and (21) in Table 2).

The causal pattern differs with regard to the relationship between changes in merger activity ($\triangle Y$) and changes in industrial output ($\triangle Q$). The regression results in Table 1 and 2 consistently show that changes in merger activity lead to changes in industrial production. The evidence suggests the following conclusions.

---

[4] The relatively low R^2 in each estimated equation is essentially due to transforming of the data by taking the first difference. A detailed discussion is given in section VI.

[5] Taking the first difference of the observed variables enables us to remove the spurious factor, i.e., the time factor. However, it does not necessarily eliminate the possibility that both stock prices and merger activity could be influenced by a third exogenous variable. Ideally, a vector auto regressive model as proposed by Mehra and Chiang [17] could be applied. However, this not only increases the degree of complexity but also creates a problem to search out an appropriate third variable to include in the model. For this reason, without loss of generality, we retained the bivariate test at this stage.

(a) a rise in merger activities leads to a decrease in real output with two years lag (see equation 15 & 19 in Table 1 & 2);
(b) there is no significant feedback relationship in reverse causation.

In order to see the significance of a group of variables, based on the estimated regressions and the resulting residuals, we constructed the F statistic to implement the Granger test and the Sims test.[6] The F statistic is calculated as follows [8,26]:

$$F= [(SSE_r - SSE_u)/(df_r - df_u)]/SSE_u/df_u \qquad (24)$$

where SSE_r and SSE_u denote, respectively, the sums of the squared errors from the estimations of the restricted and unrestricted equations; df_r and df_u are the corresponding degrees of freedom.

The calculated F statistics used for examining the causal relationship between changes in merger activity (▴Y) and the changes in stock prices (▴S) are displayed in Table 3. The evidence indicates that, when the contemporaneous terms were excluded, the null hypothesis that incremental variables do not contribute to the prediction of the variable of interest cannot be rejected, implying that there is no causal relationship between ▴Y and ▴S. The same conclusion holds true for the Sims test in which the coefficients on the future variables were found statistically insignificant. However, when current values of incremental variables were added to the system, these contemporaneous terms turn out to be statistically significant, indicating that the correlation between ▴Y and ▴S in essentially contemporaneous and displays a two way causal pattern. The evidence suggests that the iterative relationship between merger activity and the change in stock prices occurs within the current year of the time horizon.

As regards the relationship between changes in merger activity (▴Y) and movements in industrial production (▴Q), both the Granger and Sims tests reported in Table 4 consistently show that the causal relationship is running from ▴Y to ▴Q and no evidence was found on the reverse causation.

---

[6] Empirical tests of causality should concentrate on the significance of F test on a group of incremental variables or the future variables rather than the individual regression estimates.

Table 3 Tests on the Causal Relationship Between Merger
Activity and Stock Prices

Estimated Equations	Hypothesis	F Statistic	Results
Granger Test	The incremental variables equal to zero		
(Table 1)			
(5) & (6)	b(1)=b(2)=b(3)=b(4)=0	1.34	▲S≠1> ▲Y
(5) & (7)	b(0)=b(1)=b(2)=b(3)=(4)=0	6.98*	▲S=> ▲Y
(5) & (11)	B(1)=B(2)=B(3)=B(4)=0	1.35	▲Y≠> ▲S
(5) & (12)	B(0)=B(1)=B(2)=B(3)=B(4)=0	6.99*	▲Y=> ▲S
Sims Test	The future variables equal to zero		
(Table 2)			
(5) & (21)	b(1)=b(2)=b(3)=b(4)=0	2.05	▲S≠> ▲Y
(5) & (17)	B(1)=B(2)=B(3)=B(4)=0	1.42	▲Y≠> ▲S

a. * denotes significant at 5% level.

b. => denotes a causal direction; ≠> denotes no causal direction.

Table 4 Tests on the Causal Relationship Between Merger Activity

and Industrial Production

Estimated Equations	Hypothesis	F Statistic	Results
Granger Test	The incremental variables equal to zero		
(Table 1)			
(5) & (8)	$b(1)=b(2)=b(3)=b(4)=0$	0.90	$\Delta Q \not\Rightarrow \Delta Y$
(5) & (9)	$b(0)=b(1)=b(2)=b(3)=b(4)=0$	0.81	$\Delta Q \not\Rightarrow \Delta Y$
(13) & (14)	$B(1)=B(2)=B(3)=B(4)=0$	2.89*	$\Delta Y \Rightarrow \Delta Q$
(13) & (15)	$B(0)=B(1)=B(2)=B(3)=B(4)=0$	2.38*	$\Delta Y \Rightarrow \Delta Q$
Sims Test	The future variables equal to zero		
(Table 2)			
(22) & (23)	$b(1)=b(2)=b(3)=b(4)=0$	1.29	$\Delta Q \not\Rightarrow \Delta Y$
(18) & (19)	$B(1)=B(2)=B(3)=B(4)=0$	2.61*	$\Delta Y \not\Rightarrow \Delta S$

a. * denotes significant at 5% level.

b. => denotes a causal direction; ≠> denotes no causal direction.

Empirical Implication And Predictability

Our empirical analysis provides useful information in understanding the nature of the merger series and hence the model specification. The testing results in Table 3 help us to identify that the merger series, in addition to its history, is correlated with the stock prices in the contemporaneous term. This information was left out in the study by Shughart and Tollison [25]. Using the same set of merger data, they contend that merger levels are characterized by a white-noise process or by a stable first-order autoregressive scheme. Particularly, their equation can be represented by,

$$Y(t) = a + a(1)Y(t - 1) + e(t), \qquad (25)$$

where a and a (1) are parameters, and $Y(t - 1)$ is the lagged dependent variable. The principal difficulties of the Shughart and Tollison model are the failure to appreciate the influence of the extraneous information contained in the current financial markets and the exclusion of a higher order of autoregression.

In contrast to Shughart and Tollison [25], a causal model of different specification is often suggested in the literature. The simplest version of this approach assumes that merger activity relates to the state of the capital market [4, 20]. Thus,

$$Y(t) = b + b(1) S(t) + e(t) \qquad (26)$$

where b and b(1) are the parameters, and S(t) denotes current stock prices as a surrogate for the state of the capital markets. This line of argument ignores the information contained in the history of the merger variable.

To integrate expressions (25) and (26), by incorporating the information derived from Tables 3 and 4, the model is respecified as:

$$Y(t) = a+a(1) \ Y(t-1)+a(2) \ Y(t-2)+b(1) \ S(t)+e(t) \qquad (27)$$

Expressing equation (27) in a different form, we have,

$$Y(t) = a+a(1) \ \blacktriangle Y(t-1)+a(2) \ \blacktriangle Y(t-2)+b(1) \ \blacktriangle S(t)+e(t) \qquad (28)$$

The specification of equation (28) is essentially based on the information derived from the previous

Table 5 Regression Estimates of the Merger Equation

No./ Eq.	Dep. Var.	Con.	$Y(t-1)$	$Y(t-2)$	$\Delta Y(t-1)$	$\Delta Y(t-2)$	$S(t)$	$\Delta S(t)$	R^2	RMSE	F.	D.W.
				Independent Variable								
(25)	$Y(t)$	78.92	0.87*						0.76	236.5	186.2	1.25
		(1.60)	(13.64)									
(26)	$Y(t)$	248.82*					8.59*		0.41	359.8	41.1	0.35
		(3.42)					(6.40)					
(27)	$Y(t)$	64.08	1.16*	-0.48*			3.07*		0.84	200.5	94.7	1.55
		(1.44)	(10.16)	(-4.24)			(3.15)					
(28)	ΔY	-26.52			0.49*	-0.28*		18.12*	0.52	170.4	19.7	1.85
		(-1.14)			(5.01)	(2.77)		(4.97)				

NOTES:

a. Y denotes the number of mergers; S denotes the stock prices.

b. The figures in the parenthesis are statistics; D.W. denotes Durbin-Watson Statistics.

c. An asterisk (*) indicates statistically significant at the 5% level.

d. RMSE denotes Root Mean Squared Error, which is calulated on the entire sample period.

causality tests.[7] Specifically, the two order lagged merger variables and the current stock price variable are included in the equation which should be viewed as a broader version of a reduced-form equation. The specification is consistent with the optimal forecasting scheme since the choice of lagged length is derived from the empirical regularities.

Table 5 summarizes the regression estimates of equations (25) to (28). The coefficients on the right hand side variables for the estimated equations are all statistically significant. In terms of the explanatory power, all the equations perform reasonably well although equation (27) seems the most plausible.

Focusing on the empirical aspect, several comments in relation to the literature are considered in order. First, although no direct test has been performed, the evidence in Table 5 suggests that the random walk hypothesis or the AR(1) process proposed by Shughart and Tollison [25] should be rejected because the second order lagged merger variable is statistically significant. Note that the evidence presented here is consistent with the finding provided Clark, Chakrabarti, and Chiang [5], where they found the merger series follows an AR(2) process.

Second, equations (27) and (28) constitute integrated models that combine both autoregressive terms and causal factors, indicating that either univariate time series models suggested by Shughart and Tollison [25], Clark, Chakrabarti and Chiang [5] or purely causal models Nelson, Steiner, Chappel and Cheng [28,20,4] appear to be special cases.

Third, although equations (25) to (27) yield higher R squared, the spurious correlation and serial correlation suggests that equation (28) is the most acceptable version. The empirical evidence indicates that the merger series without removing the time factor tends to yield a higher R squared and generates biased estimates.

---

[7] Since earlier tests indicate that contemporaneous two-way causation exists between stock prices and merger activity, a so-called simultaneous equation problem may appear in equation (28). To remove this bias, one might have to construct a larger econometric model, which is beyond the scope of this study.

Finally, with respect to predictability, the evidence clearly shows that equation (28) out-performs all other equations. This is evidenced by the smallest RMSE in Table 5. The out-of-sample fit reported in Table 6 manifests this result. The superiority of equation (28) is due to the fact that we effectively exploit the information underlying the merger series and hence provide more accurate specification of the model.

To sum up, the merger series itself is nonstationary and follows an AR(2) process although the series per se is stochastic in nature. We can assert with a high level of confidence that stock prices contain useful information of an explanatory nature relating to merger activity.

Summary And Conclusion

Our analysis found a significant contemporaneous relationship between merger activity in manufacturing and mining and the S & P Stock Price Index. This confirms Nelson's results. We do not assert, however, that stock market prices cause acceleration or deceleration in merger activity. Rather, as suggested by Gort, stock price movements create conditions favorable or unfavorable to merger activity [7]. For example, in a rising stock market, the cost of replacement assets may exceed the market price of existing assets, thereby encouraging growth by combination. Yet setting the stage does not assume the play will go on. Examination of the data shows periods when rising prices did not elicit comparable increases in merger activity. Other variables - technological, institutional and behavioral -- also affect merger activity.

On the other hand, an increase in merger activity gives added impetus to a rising stock market. Rumors of a takeover generally set off an upward movement in the stock prices of companies attractive to potential acquisitiors. Also, mergers are mostly executed with premiums ranging 20 to 60 percent above market. The flow of forces generates a reciprocal influence between

Table 6 The Predictability of Various Merger Equations

Equation	Dependent Variable	Independent Variable	Observation	Actual Value	Predicted Value	RMSE
(25)	Y(t)	Y(t-1)	57	439	609	93.41
			58	559	462	
			59	590	567	
			60	514	594	
			61	519	527	
(26)	Y(t)	S(t)	57	439	988	558.93
			58	559	1125	
			59	590	1092	
			60	514	1093	
			61	519	1132	
(27)	Y(t)	Y(t-1), Y(t-2), S(t)	57	439	609	182.67
			58	559	594	
			59	590	800	
			60	514	771	
			61	519	689	
(28)	ΔY(t)	ΔY(t-1), ΔY(t-2), ΔS(t)	57	439	547	84.21
			58	559	697	
			59	590	569	
			60	514	505	
			61	519	589	

Notes: RMSE is calculated by holding last five observations.

stock prices and merger activity.[8]

The relationship between merger activity in manufacturing and mining and the Index of Industrial Production is ambiguous. Here our results show a rise in merger activity leads to a decrease in real output with a two year lag. The point merits further investigation. It may reflect defensive mergers in a sector of the economy declining in relative importance or the deficiency in the data which excludes banking and the service industries. However, given the time span covered in the analysis (1919-1979), it also raises the issue of whether business combinations have a net adverse effect on real output, that is, real output may be less than optimal as the number of mergers in an industry increases.

---

[8] Although the closeness of the event does not allow for appropriate investigation, the recent break in N.Y. Stock Exchange does apparently support the interpretation of an interaction between stock prices and merger activity. Based upon an interview with John Gerlach, Associate Director of Mergers and Acquisitions; Bear, Sterns; November 12, 1987.

References

[1]   Box, George P. and Gwilym M Jenkins. _Time Series Analysis_, _Forecasting and Control_. San Francisco: 1976.

[2]   Bradley, James W. and Donald H. Korn. _Acquisitions and Corporate Development_. Lexington, Mass: D.C. Heath, 1981.

[3]   Carleton, Willard; T. Harris; J. Roberts; J. Stewart. _An Empirical Study of Merger Activities_. Washington, D.C.: Federal Trade Commission, 1978.

[4]   Chappell, Henry W. and David C. Cheng, "Firms' Acquisition Decisions and Tobin's Q Ratio," _Journal of Economics and Business_ 36, 29-42 (1984).

[5]   Clark, John J., Alok K. Chakrabarti, and Thomas C. Chiang, "Trend and Stochastic Movements in U.S. Merger Activity." _Quarterly Review of Business and Economics_, 1988, forth-coming.

[6]   Cowling, Keith; O. Stoneman; J. Cubbin; J. Cable; B. Hall; S. Domberger; P. Dutton, _Mergers and Economic Performance_. Cambridge University Press, 1980.

[7]   Gort, Michael. "An Economic Disturbance Theory of Mergers." _Quarterly Journal of Economics_, Vol. 83, No. 4 (November 1969).

[8]   Granger, C.W.J. "Investigating Causal Relations by Econometric Models and Cross-Spectral Methods." _Econometrica_, Vol. 37 (July 1969), pp. 424-38.

[9]   Haugh, Larry D. "Checking the Independence of Two Covariance--Stationary Time Series: A Univariate Residual Cross-Correlation Approach." _Journal of the American Statistical Association_, Vol. 71 (June 1976), pp. 378-85.

[10] Hayes, Robert H. and William J. Abernathy. "Managing Our Economy to Decline." _Harvard Business Review_, Vol. 58, No. 4 (July-August 1980).

[11] Hsiao, Cheng. "Autoregressive Modeling and Money-Income Causality Detection." _Journal of Monetary Economics_, 7(1981) pp. 85-106.

[12] Khan, Mohsin. "Inflation and International Reserves: A Time- Series Analysis." _Staff Papers_, International Monetary Fund, Vol.26, No.4 (December 1979), pp. 69-724.

[13] Leontiades, Milton. "Rationalizing the Unrelated Acquisition." _California Management Review_, Vol.24, No. 3, 1982.

[14] Lynch, Harry. _Financial Performance of Conglomerates_. Cambridge, Mass.: Harvard University Press, 1971.

[15] Mandelker, G. "Risk and Return: The Case of Merging Firms." _Journal of Financial Economics_, (December 1984), pp. 303-335.

[16] Manne, Henry G. "Merger and the Market for Corporate Control." _Journal of Political Economy_, Vol. 73, No. 2, April 1965).

[17] Mehra, Yash P. and Thomas C. Chiang. "Tests of Exogeneity and Causality Specifications in Monetary Models of Exchange Rate Determination." _Atlantic Economic Journal_, (July 1984).

[18] Mueller, Dennis C. "A Theory of Conglomerate Mergers." _Quarterly Journal of Economics_, Vol. 83, No. 4 (November 1969).

[19] Mueller, Dennis C. ed. _The Determinants and Effects of Mergers_. Cambridge, Mass.: Oelgeschlager, Gunn and Haines,1980.

[20] Nelson, Richard L. _Merger Movements in American Industry_: 1895-1956. Princeton: Princeton University Press, 1959.

[21] Pierce, David A. and Larry D. Haugh. "Causality in Temporal Systems: Characterization and a Survey."_Journal of Econometrics_, Vol. 5 (August 1977), pp.265-93.

[22] Reich, Robert B. _The Next American Frontier_. New York: Time Books, 1983.

[23] Salter, Malcolm S. and Wolf A. Weinhold. _Diversification Through Acquisitions: Strategies for Creating Economic Value_. New York: Free Press, 1979.

[24] Schwert, G. William. "Test of Causality: The Message in the Innovations." in _Three Aspects of Policy and Policy Making: Data and Institutions_, ed. by Karl Brunner and Allan H. Meltzer, Carnegie-Rochester Conference Series on Public Policy, Vol. 10 (Amsterdam 1979), pp. 55-96.

[25] Shughart II, William F. and Robert D. Tollison, "The Random Character of Merger Activity." _Rand Journal of Economics_, Vol. 15, No. 4 (Winter 1984).

[26] Sims, Christopher A. "Money, Income and Causality." _American Economic Review_, (September 1972), pp. 540-52.

[27] Souder, William E. and Alok K. Chakrabarti. "Acquisitions: Do They Really Work Out?" _Interface_, Vol. 14, No. 4 (July-August 1984).

[28] Steiner, Peter O. _Mergers_, Ann Arbor: University of Michigan Press, 1977.

[29] Stigler, George J. "Monopoly and Oligopoly by Merger." _American Economic Review_, Vol. 40, No. 2, 1950.

[30] Zellner, Arnold. "Causality and Econometrics." In _Three Aspects of Policy and Policy Making: Knowledge, Data and Institutions_, ed. by Karl Brunner and Allan K. Meltzer, Carnegie-Rochester Conference Series on Public Policy, Vol. 10 (Amsterdam 1979), pp. 9-54.

MERGERS & ACQUISITIONS:A CLASSICAL TALE

by

Douglas F. Mayer[1]

Mergers and acquisitions, takeovers hostile or friendly are not new phenomena. The purchase of or raid on one company by another did not begin with Willian Agee's attempted takeover of Martin Marietta in 1982. Such activity was old when the raiders of the 1920's pooled their resources to buy up huge blocks of stock, drive up prices, and then retreat with huge profits (Smith & Sandler, 11/10/86, p.47). This popular theme was not new when the robber barons of the 1870's and 80's ruthlessly compelled companies in their way to sell out or be destroyed. Takeovers-- essentially corporate takeovers -- are as old as western civilization.

Indeed, takeovers were old hat by the forth century B.C., when Alexander the Great conquered all of Persia. By then the whole Middle East had been conquered several times. The takeover artists were those tribes who had the resources and the perceived need to dispatch their neighbors. But it was Alexander who raised the art of the takeover to new heights. The trick, as Alexander discovered, was not how to do a takeover, but how to run the newly acquired country.

Similarly, Julius Caesar also knew the art of takeover and control. It was he who enlarged the Roman Empire to the north and west, by conquering Gaul and England. Caesar's skill was not only in conquest, but managing his troops for the takeover, and having complete loyalty in his ranks. Like Alexander, he knew that movement ahead was dependent on a strong support system at headquarters and throughout the organization. Caesar knew that a flashy campaign in Gaul was a brilliant antidote to a bad press at home.

Finally, Niccolo Machiavelli, the 16th Century Florentine, provided a bridge to modern takeover theory with his classic, The Prince, published in 1512. His advice to the rulers of the early of the early modern Italian city states about how takeovers were to be accomplished was direct and certain. He was the one

---

[1] Associate Professor of Management at Hartwick College

who listed the steps and the reasons for them; he condensed the experience of earlier acquisitors into a handbook, a 16th Century policy manual.

Each of these notable men offered important insights about leading takeovers, and managing then afterwards. Their knowledge is being rediscovered today as modern observers of the corporate takeover world describe the successes and failures of contemporary corporate raiders. This paper will explore some of the lessons that Alexander, Julius Caesar and Machiavelli offer for those contemplating a takeover, or faced with the problem of managing a company just acquired. In many ways this paper is a visit -- like the recent movie --Back to the Future.

WHAT THEY DID AND WHY:

T. Boone Pickens only attacks those companies that seem to him to be vulnerable. When performance is inadequate, when stock is undervalued, when management numbers deem bloated, he moves in. Carl Icahn makes similar statements. In a recent interview he said: "In corporate management anti-Darwinian patterns have evolved over the last twenty years: survival of the unfittest." (Powell, 1986)

Mismanagement may be the stated rationale for beginning a takeover. It is more likely that a choice opportunity cannot be turned down -- like the chance to swipe a warm cookie. Machiavelli noted that opportunity and resources were the keys to successful takeovers. Power, defined as money, skill, or both, are the necessary ingredients for conquest. According to W.W. Tarn, "Alexander's invaded Persia [because] he never thought of not doing it; it was his inheritance." (Tarn, 1964, p.8) Indeed, Alexander's father, Phillip commented: "O my son, look thee out a kingdom equal to and worthy of thyself, for Macedonia is too little for thee." (Plutarch, 1952, p.543) Put bluntly, there was little reason for him to conquer all that he did, except that it was there.

Julius Caesar (100-44 B.C.) was one Roman Emperor given to takeovers. Part of the reason for this was Alexander, who was an inspiration for Caesar.

At Cadiz he saw a statue of Alexander the Great in the Temple of Hercules, and was overheard to sigh impatiently: vexed, it seems, that at an age when Alexander had already conquered the whole world, he himself had done nothing in the least epoch-making. (Suetonius, 1957, p.12)

Caesar proceeded to conquer Gaul and Great Britain. The reasons for his conquests were not very clear, at least to Suetonius, but he was successful:

> He ... lost no opportunity of picking quarrels-- however flimsy the pretext -- with allies as well as hostile and barbarous tribes, and marching against them ....
> Briefly, his nine years of governorship (of Gaul) produced the following results. He reduced to the form of a province the whole of gaul enclosed by the Pyrenees, the Alps, the Cevennes, the Rhine, and the Rhone... and after that Great Britain. (Suetonius, 1957, p.19)

Certainly Caesar's self confessed need to emulate Alexander is one reason for his adventurism. Caesar was not altogether popular, especially with Roman politicians; the Gallic campaign was reported by both Suetonius and Plutarch as being popular with the citizenry, and was a means of keeping the home politicians on the defensive. He had a good time leading an army and bashing barbarian heads. Like Alexander, conquest was Caesar's destiny; unlike Alexander, Caesar needed his conquests to be welcomed in Rome.

Machiavelli offers his own insights on why takeovers happen. For him, "why" is not a question; such things do happen. The acquisitive desire is natural, and when the prince has enough power and ability to fulfill this desire he does not need any other justification. The important and exciting thing is what becomes of the takeover. It is that subject which will be considered next.

POST TAKEOVER: MAINTAINING CONTROL

What to do after the merger is accomplished is a hard question. Recent takeover history is not a compendium of success stories. In fact, even when a takeover is friendly, there is little to suggest that life will be smooth for the combined businesses. When Fluor took over St. Joe Minerals, the parent company promised to keep hands off St. Joe's management. Instead, Fluor overmanaged and smothered the new acquisition. What might have been a good fit turned into a disaster because the boss knew best, and failed

to respect the management strengths of St. Joe.
(Prokesch, 1985, p.92)

It is instructive to examine what Alexander did
after his conquests. As he proceeded to roll over
tribes and civilizations in Asia Minor (present day
Turkey, Iraq, Iran, Pakistan, and other countries of
the middle east) he worked hard to assimilate them. He
was adamant that they not be alienated, but that they
accept his domination without rancor. Thus, newly
conquered territory was encouraged to keep its local
structure culture. In spite of Aristotle's teaching--
that all others were subservient to Greeks--
Alexander admired the way the Persians organized, and
he decided to rule with them, rather than over them.

The trick was doing this. It is easy to direct
lieutenants to adopt the ways of the newly won prize,
but it is a hard order to operationalize. Alexander
demonstrated what he meant by requiring his leaders to
adopt local customs and to wear native dress. He
believed that by setting the example, the boss could
implement a policy of joint governance, and what better
example that showing intent by dressing like the
natives. Plutarch wrote:

> ...[Alexander] marched into Parthia (an
> ancient country southeast of the Caspain
> Sea], where not having much to do, he first
> put on the barbaric dress, perhaps with the
> view of making the work of civilizing them
> easier, as nothing gains more upon men than a
> conformity to their fashions and customs.
> At first he wore this habit only when he
> conversed with the barbarians, or within
> doors, among his intimate friends and
> companions, but afterwards he appeared in it
> abroad, when he rode out, and at public
> audiences. (1952, p. 562)

Clearly Alexander's strategy was not compulsion, but
assimilation. He did not want to rule only by fear,
but by demonstrating interest in those he conquered,
and respecting their ways. Plutarch reported:

> ... he more and more accommodated himself in
> his way of living to that of the natives, and
> tried to bring them also as near as he could
> to the Macedonian customs, wisely considering
> that whilst he was engaged in an expedition
> which would carry him far from thence it
> would be wiser to depend upon good-will which

might arise from intermixture and association as a means of maintaining tranquility, than upon force and compulsion. (1952, p.563)

This strategy paid off, for Alexander was revered. And being revered was no surprise when the boss was as generous as Alexander. Upon conquering a small country in present day India, the local leader asked how he and his fellow countrymen might earn Alexander's friendship. Alexander's response: "I would have them choose you to govern them." Alexander understood that managing a takeover depended on having the respect and trust of the new addition. He recognized that others had ability, that the Persians were fantastic organizers, and that by offering them respect, he could administer far larger territories than would be possible by fear and recrimination.

Carl Icahn's takeover of TWA might be considered "Alexandrian." His bid was successful, in part, because of his willingness to work with trade unions at TWA. He professed an interest in accepting them and working with them to assure that TWA would survive. So far, TWA has performed better with a more symbiotic relationship of management and unions. (It should be noted, however, that Icahn was willing to go along with the unions only up to a point: the Flight Attendants found out the hard way that Icahn could be tough.) Icahn is attempting to take over USX (formerly United States Steel) by a similar wooing of the Steelworkers' Union. (Powell, 1986)

Other takeover artists might learn from Alexander. GM bought Ross Perot's EDS in order to support its own need for increased computer capability. The idea on paper was fantastic: EDS provided a boost to GM in many ways --Computer support, good returns, technical and product excellence and compatibility, not to mention Perot as an addition to the GM board. But the cultures of the two were very different. Assimilation proved elusive for the acquisitor, who did not comprehend the EDS culture of a strict dress and conduct code which precluded beards and **any** martini lunches. The EDS managers, assigned the task of bringing GM data processing people up to speed, appeared arrogant and demeaning. Some of the GM Data Processing sites were faced with unionization campaigns; some 600 division employees left rather than transfer to the EDS division. (Business Week, 1985, p.118) In retrospect, it seems clear that had the EDS managers assigned to GM been 'Alexandrian", they might well have adopted some of the norms of the GM operation. THe kind of assimilation that Alexander demonstrated offered opportunities to those he conquered -- opportunities to maintain their self respect, to teach their new bosses about them, and to develop mutual respect for new relationships and a new organization.

Assimilation is not the only way a takeover can be run. Alexander capitalized on the resources in the territories he conquered; but that is not irrefutable proof that such leadership always works. Julius Caesar did not subscribe to Alexander's approach, even though Alexander was his model. Unlike Alexander, he did not treat the newly acquired territories with magnanimity; he was harsh and cruel. Caesar depended on his own soldiers to control the conquered territories. His strategy was to have deep support from his own people. Plutarch wrote:

> He was so much master of the good-will and hearty service of his soldiers that those who in other expeditions were but ordinary men displayed a courage past defeating or withstanding when they went upon any danger where Caesar's glory was concerned... This love of honor and passion for distinction were inspired into them and cherished in them by Caesar himself, who by his unsparing distribution of money and honors, showed them that he did not heap up wealth from the wars for his own luxury, .., but that all he received was but a public fund laid by for the reward and encouragement of valor ... Added to this also, there was no danger to which he did not willingly expose himself, no labor from which he pleaded an exemption. (Plutarch, 1952, p.583)

Caesar was a great leader and motivator. His strategy remains popular. For example, when General Electric bought NBC in 1986, Welch, GE's Chairman immediately placed his own lieutenant at NBC's helm. Lawrence Tisch behaved similarly when he took over CBS. THese men know what Caesar knew -- that to hold tight control over newly won territory people loyal to and dependent on the boss are the key.

In fact Alexander used his conquered people for support and strength. Caesar depended entirely on his own soldiers. Both understood the importance of leading and delegating. Each offers a distinct model for dealing with the acquired company after it has been won.

Niccolo Machiavelli offered advice about managing a takeover after the victory of conquest. He was convinced that the key to successful control lay in eradicating the former leadership. He wrote:

> To hold them securely, it is enough to have extinguished the line of princes who ruled them formerly and to maintain pre-existent conditions. When there is no change in customs, men will live quietly. Anyone who conquers such territories and wishes to hold onto them must do two things: the first is to extinguish the ruling family; the second is to alter neither the laws nor the taxes. Thus in a short time they will become one with the conqueror's original possessions. (1981, pp.15-16)

Changing the top level executives is simple for Machiavelli, as it was with Caesar. THeir advice was the same: put people in place that are loyal vassals, ready to do your biding. It is unusual, though, for an acquirer to follow the second part of Machiavelli's dictum: leave things alone. Beatrice Foods bought Esmark, but could not keep its hands off. For example, Beatrice management ordered the Beatrice logo onto Playtex Division packaging. The result was an internecine war about labels on wrappers that hurt the business. (<u>Business Week</u>, 8/19/84, p.34)

Machiavelli was aware that sometimes mergers occur between vastly different kinds of organizations. His advice:

> When a state accustomed to live in freedom under its own laws is acquired, there are three ways of keeping it: the first is to destroy it; the second is to go and live there in person; the third is to continue to let it live under its own laws, taking tribute from it, and setting up a government composed of a few men who will keep it friendly to you. Such a government, being the creature of the Prince, will be aware that it cannot survive without his friendship and support, and it will do everything to maintain his authority. A city which is used to its own freedom is more easily controlled by means of its own citizens than by any other, provided one chooses not to destroy it. (1981, p.24)

The first solution --destruction-- is one that corporate raiders sometimes use after acquisition. They work to sell off the assets in order to in order to maintain cash flow to service the debt. This was

the fear when Chevron and Gulf contemplated merging.
The Wall Street Journal reported that "The
consolidation plan would nearly dismember Gulf." (1984)
Similarly, it is unusual for CEOs to go live at the
newly acquired division in North Dakota; they could not
afford to lose touch with the Westchester headquarters.
So Machiavelli's third suggestion of 'colonizing' seems
to be the most practical. This was the strategy that
Alexander used.   Caesar used his army as the
colonizers, without working for the assimilation that
Alexander tried to achieve.

CONCLUSION:

        The last has yet to be written on corporate
mergers and acquisitions, hostile or friendly.   But,
the stories that have been in the business press on the
subject recently are only the latest installments in a
very long serial.   What a reading of the classics can
bring to understanding mergers and acquisitions is the
sharpness of a story well told, with clear heroes and
consequences, with a richness of detail, imagery and
metaphor.   It is the stories of such men that provide
simple and clear direction for the thoughtful reader.
And while the direction may be simple and clear, the
execution of a plan will be difficult.   Alexander knew
that, as did Julius Caesar. Machiavelli knew it too.

SELECTED READINGS

Alter, J. "Civil War at CBS" <u>Newsweek</u> 9/15/86 pp46-50

Levin,D. "Fearing Takeover of gulf oil, Employees Are
Showing Myriad Symptoms of Stress", <u>Wall
Street Journal</u>, 2/28/86, pp. 34-35.

Machiavelli, N. <u>The Prince</u>, Airmont Publishing, 1965

Miles, G. "Icahn had USX Boxed In", <u>Business Week</u>,
10/20/86, pp.24-26.

Plutarch, <u>The Lives of the Noble Grecians and Romans</u>,
Chicago: Encyclopedia Britannica, 1952.

Powell, W and Friday, C. "The MAn of Steel", <u>Newsweek</u>,
10/20/86, pp.50-53.

Suetonius, <u>The Twelve Caesars</u> Baltimore, MD: Penguin
1957.

MERGERS IN HIGHER EDUCATION

by

Michael P. Murphy[1]

"I am convinced that the most effective political strategy for higher education during a period of declining enrollment is to join forces in a coordinated effort to achieve support for the entire enterprise, not support for special interests within higher education. In effect, I am suggesting that all of us in higher education circle the wagon and shoot out rather than in, as has been our practice."

Richard D. Wagner
Illinois Board of Higher Education

"It is treacherous terrain."

Price Pritchett
After the Merger

"The strong survive and the weak become merged."

Joan B. Cannon
The Organizational and Human
Implications of Mergers

The conditions that bring about mergers in higher education appear on first examination different enough from those in the profit sector that they have sometimes eluded similar scrutiny and are little written about. Part of this difference may be accounted for by the persistent perception, even in the midst of college closings, that higher education is somehow "exempt from the inevitable law of supply and demand." (Crossland, 1980) However, as colleges and universities seek to diversify in the face of increased competition for credit and non-credit programs, the

---

[1] Director of the College of St. Thomas in Minneapolis, and former Acting Academic Dean of the College of St. Catherine, St. Paul, Minnesota

acquisition of already-existing institutions may be seen as the most timely _entre_ into a new field.

Another part of the dilemma in higher education over merger is knowing when to act. O'Neill and Barnett (1980, p.7) cited one trustee's frustration over such a possibility. "This college has been in financial difficulty for 125 years. How am I to know that God won't provide and see it through yet another year?"

Quite apart from the exigencies of divine intervention, it is possible to identify trends in the development of educational mergers, and common characteristics, (pre- and post-merger) which lead or have lead to such activity. In the seminal work in the field, Millett (1976) concluded that higher education mergers in the 1960's came about because of the desire to build a strengthened university and cities, for example, the acquisition by SUNY of the University of Buffalo and the absorption of the University of Kansas City into the University of Missouri system. In the 1970's, however, such activity, according to Millett, might be better understood as efforts to deal with financial stringency, as was the case in the Polytechnic Institute of New York merger and that of Western College and Miami University of Ohio. The pattern for the 1980's is not yet clear; however, it might perhaps be understood best from this vantage point as a combination of financial stringency and diversification.

Separate from these general trends, specific factors giving rise to educational mergers sometimes grow out of unique local conditions. In the case of Tennessee State University and University of Tennessee-Nashville, both institutions were under a court-ordered mandate to overcome segregation through merger. (Matlock and Humphries, 1979; Shimeall, 1980) And the Case Institute of Technology-Western College merger was described as an effort at improved economies in the long run and hope of creating quality educational programming in the Cleveland area. (Fisher, 1978) John Millis, former president of Case Institute prior to the merger, also described that event as "the first shotgun marriage of two educational institutions in the history of America." (Fisher, p. 38) Somervill (1983) notes, however, that to a great extent, mergers were not motivated primarily by pressure external to the institutions.

Achieving economies of scale has been described among others as a primary reason for the stronger school's involvement in a merger. (O'Neill & Barnett, 1980)

> The strategy of the stronger school must be to maximize the ability to serve society's needs by securing enrollment increases, energy-efficient facilities, property and endowment while minimizing such liability as debt, tenured faculty who duplicate rather than complement existing (programs) energy-wasteful facilities, etc.. (p. 28)

Somervill (1983, p. 1) sees expansion and the promise of "the upward quality of institutional programs" as motivating factors in educational mergers. Barr (1985, p. 52) also notes that the merger of academic departments or schools within separate institutions could lead to "greater institutional security, improved programming, and expanded opportunities for students." Somervill (1983, p. 4) concludes that "the relationship between enrollments and economics had the greatest potential for contributing to the merger discussions."

Motivation for the acquiring institutions may be driven by horizontal diversification. For the struggling prospective partner, however, merger may be the best mechanism short of closure for that Board of Trustees to exercise its responsibility and insure that some measure of the institution's mission might be preserved. However, O'Neill and Barnett found that the "reality of the merger may turn out to be less attractive than surface appearances would warrant." (1980, p. 25) Millet found, too, that educational "merger in an atmosphere of financial exigency is likely to be less well planned, less open, less satisfactory to the persons most concerned with the consequences." (1976, p. 52)

The unexpected results of educational mergers might derive in some sense from the impression that the transaction is made to look like something it is not. Citing merger transactions in all sectors, Cannon (1983) quotes one participant as indicating that:

> Many acquisitions in fact are made to look and sound like mergers--mergers are never made to sound like acquisitions. Mergers enjoy great societal acceptability, and can be made to look benevolent and highly

beneficial to the community and to the consumer. Acquisitions by their very acquisitive title, are the more difficult to justify in social terms (p. 5)

Cannon's observation may be over-strong in assessing merger vs. acquisition language in higher education and the community reaction to it. However, the stronger institution may in fact want to project an image of growth in difficult times by making such a move.

O'Neill and Barnett (1980) are helpful in providing more precise language describing the spectrum of inter-institutional cooperation as follows:

Federation--Two or more institutions retain their corporate identities but agree to surrender to a central administration a measure of autonomy in the overall management of the combined institutions. (p. 18)

Affiliation is described as the connection that may exist between two related organizations, as is true in the juxtaposition between a "church body and the college it sponsors" (p. 18)

Merger is seen as a combination of two or more institutions, while a consolidated merger is described as existing when "two or more corporations dissolve their respective legal identities and become a wholly new corporation carrying forth all the properties and obligations of the former corporations." (O'Neill and Barnett, p. 20)

Finally, in a dissolution/acquisition, agreement emerges "under which one institution is legally dissolved and its assets and liabilities are acquired with court approval by the surviving institution." (O'Neill and Barnett, p. 20)

Technically speaking, then, that form of institutional combination under examination in this paper is the dissolution/acquisition, and under this condition pre- and post- merger impacts are generally more pronounced than in less extreme efforts at cooperation.

Factors to consider in such negotiations within higher education include those described earlier as well as:

1. Market and constituent receptivity;
2. Conflict of institutional cultures--especially where separate missions were quite distinct;
3. Transferability of credit;
4. The extent of internal involvement in discussions;
5. Professional Accrediting agencies & affiliations;
6. State approval and the need for Board involvement in the merger.

Regarding the latter according to Peters, "A significant negative correlation was found between the extent of participation of the Board and the overall results indicator....the greater the participation of the Board, the more favorable the perceived results." (Peters, p. 209)

In post-merger situations generally there occurs what has been called the "decoupling of responsibility and power" (Fisher, p. 42), or perhaps more appropriately a sense of loss of local autonomy--certainly more pronounced in the acquired institution but creating dissonance throughout the new, now more complex, organization. (Cannon, 1983; Blake and Srygley Mouton, 1984) It appears to me no less true in higher education than in other sectors.

Doubt and organizational ambiguity can be persistent (Gale, 1986) and widespread. According to Bastien (1986),

A change of ownership or top management is among the most traumatic of organizational changes, and generates a mood of profound uncertainty...the typical response to this type of uncertainty is for the manager to focus on personal security rather than on organizational goals....(p.10)

There develops a common reaction of self-protection - ironically at precisely the point in the post-merger scenario when redoubled efforts in the face of the new challenge are expected and necessary. According to Bastien and Van DeVen (1985), "the longer and more intensely this uncertainty is present, the greater the likelihood of turnover among managers and professionals in the acquired firm." (p. 33)

In addition to the almost natural anxiety that grows out of post-merger ambiguity, often the magnitude and complexity of the task have been underestimated.

147

(Peters, 1977)   Often, too, poor follow-up management
leads to neglect.   According to Pritchett (1985),
"...while there was good negotiation, there is bad
integration."

> The delicate footwork manifested in the
> sensitive process of making the deal
> disappears. Parent company management may
> breathe a sigh of relief with the opportunity
> to get back to 'business as usual.'   But
> people in the acquired firm know its a new
> ball game....the new owner ....characterist-
> ically quits tiptoeing too soon. (p. 25)

Difficulties emerge in the post-merger period
because of a sometimes subtle, unselfconscious
arrogance that enters the scene.   Blake and Srygley
Mouton (1984) found that:

> Members of the acquiring organization often
> think they have a far greater understanding
> of the workings of the acquired organization
> than they actually do and do not realize they
> are considered to be uninformed and ignorant
> by members of that organization.   This
> further reduces chances for collaboration
> between members of the two organizations.
> Finally, when those in the organization being
> acquired remain reticent, hesitant, or
> remote, they may be viewed as withholding
> help when spontaneous contributions should be
> forthcoming. (p. 42)

Finally, in the sorting out that takes place after
the merger, a kind of "merger politics" develops.
Somervill (1983) found that political factions emerged
out of the "...centralization of decision-making
following the merger, the perceived need to become more
influential on campus, and the perceived need to
improve the internal management of the unit." (p. 8)

With these dynamics in mind, I'd like to turn
briefly now to consideration of the recent acquisition
of St. Mary's Junior College (Minneapolis) by the
College of St. Catherine (St. Paul).

Founded in the early 1960's by the Sisters of St.
Joseph, the co-educational junior college derived a
mission in health and human services at the certificate
and associate's degree levels in such areas as nursing,
occupational therapy, health care interpreting,
respiratory therapy and medical records management. In

addition, St. Mary's Junior College (SMJC) maintained a particular emphasis in service to the economically, educationally and physically disadvantaged student. It had developed a range of special learning and advising services, a non-punitive grading policy, and a liberal arts base inherent in all of its degree programs.

Enrollment at the junior college had peaked in the late 1970's and early 1980's at nearly 1,000 students but had begun to decline dramatically over recent years because of the lack of interest in its associate degree nursing program--the college's largest.

Alarmed by this fall-off of interest in nursing, and seeking affiliation with a 4-year degree granting institution to broaden its educational base, SMJC's administration with the approval of its Board devised an exploratory affiliation document which it circulated to two other local private, Catholic 4-year institutions. The first, St. Thomas College, is a co-educational diocesan school with an enrollment, undergraduate and graduate, of approximately 5,000 students. The second, the College of St. Catherine, is a liberal arts college for women and, like St. Mary's Junior College, supported by the Sisters of St. Joseph. Its enrollment is approximately 2,500 students.

Three-way exploratory discussions were carried on for a short time until St. Thomas College withdrew from them, citing its up-coming merger-related talks with a nearby seminary and the observation that the more natural historic and programmatic connection existed between the other two schools.

The College of St. Catherine (CSC) was founded in the early 1900's and increased numbers in recent years by its special programs for returning adult women in day and weekend programs. Such diversification had allowed CSC a measure of stability in a period of increasing competition for the traditional-age student particularly. Yet while the total number of CSC students was increasing annually, that number sometimes disguised a shift toward the older, part-time learner. Consequently, despite the introduction of new certificate programs and a graduate program in organizational management, credit hours generated at CSC remained constant in recent years, and interest in its 4-year nursing program--long a great strength--had begun to fall off. In 1982-3, CSC suffered an unexpected enrollment decline of about 100+ students and implemented a series of cutbacks and freezes to manage programs within budget. The college is highly dependent on tuition income, highly tenured, and generates marginal fund balances annually.

Early on in the negotiations, CSC engaged the services of consultants in educational mergers; and once it was clear that CSC was interested in exploring alternatives for affiliation with SMJC, a joint committee of faculty, administrators and Board members was created by the Presidents of both institutions. Considerable efforts were made by the Presidents and by this merger executive committee to maintain an atmosphere of openness and equity in discussions. Despite these efforts, however, talks stalled over SMJC's interest in retaining local programmatic control while expanding such programs into bachelor and master's degree levels under the auspices of the senior level college. For their part, CSC representatives feared the use of the degree granting power alone without insuring quality control by its faculty or continuity of program. Later, a greater fear was to emerge about the blurring of traditional marketing appeals of both institutions by blending them too closely without distinction.

The SMJC representatives feared absorption by CSC in a process that might rob the junior college of its special focus. More particularly, SMJC feared the loss of its topdown entrepreneurial ability to identify new market needs and implement programs in dramatic fashion. The decision-making style at the senior level college was perceived as slow, deliberative and consensus-based.

Several weeks into the negotiations the groups reached an impasse--where the senior college resisted the access the junior college insisted on in the development of its new programs. The advantages to the senior college in the proposed cooperation simply were not clear.

The CSC contingent reported this difficulty to its president and suggested that if talks were to continue, a merger/acquisition was recommended. In their proposal, the junior college would be taken over by the senior college, thus assuring a measure of control. But the special thrust of the junior college's mission would be preserved.

The CSC president and Board approved this strategy and a proposal was made to and accepted by the junior college.

Now in the negotiation process, merger-related information recommended by Millet (1976) was collected on both institutions and examined by the merger executive committee. Such issues as the current operating and enrollment situation were reviewed, as were the current state of academic competition, the condition of short and long term planning at both colleges, and the state of academic leadership. Each college developed a list of non-negotiable areas. For the junior college, as might be expected, it centered on holding fast to the issues of access and mission. For the senior college, the women-only nature of the four year institution was non-debatable, as was its emphasis on selectivity in the admissions process.

On analysis, it appeared that the merger would not represent short-term dramatic improvement in enrollment. However, inasmuch as the Sister community was willing to gift the junior college to CSC, the action did not signify sizeable risk.

Negotiations proceeded, with communication to both campus communities coordinated in content and released jointly. The merger executive committee created 8-10 joint task force of staff and faculty to examine and report back on such issues as: transfer of credit; schedule; salaries and benefits; joint programming; tuition and fees; public relations, alumnae relations; space and facilities; and corporate cultures. The committee itself examined legal implications, merger related expenses, transfer of financial aid funds, accreditation and associational issues.

An Intent to Merge document was signed in early Fall 1985. This document identified the direction negotiations were taking in areas under continuing discussion. The purposes of the Intent document was to demonstrate to the colleges' constituencies the seriousness of the discussions and to imply that if outstanding issues were settled to the satisfaction of both administrations and Boards, the merger would proceed. The final decisions were to be made at the colleges' upcoming Board meetings.

In October 1985, the SMJC Board approved-- providing similar approval by the CSC Board--the conditions of the merger/acquisition which called for the dissolution of its corporation and the assumption of its assets and liabilities, and degree-granting authority, by CSC. Further, the proposal called for an administrative consolidation under the CSC Board and president, the maintenance where possible of the unique mission of the junior college campus (which would be referred to as the St. Mary's Campus of the College of St. Catherine). And while consolidations were called for in staff offices, the two faculties would remain separate, with individual salary scales, handbooks and program approval authority within their current scope. Gradually, however, it was hoped that faculty would affiliate over departmentally-based joint programming possibilities.

At the Board meeting of November 1985, the CSC faculty representatives presented the Board members with a petition signed by a majority of the college's full-time faculty. The petition argued against the merger on basis of the need to preserve academic quality, and the goal of protecting the liberal arts nature of the institution without appearing to turn in very uncertain times to a particular emphasis in the health and human services areas. In addition, the associate degree in nursing at the junior college was seen as antithetical to the baccalaureate-based program at CSC.

Persuaded that the merger represented an opportunity to expand the CSC presence in Minneapolis, and that merged resources might allow for creative, market-sensitive joint programming, the Board approved the merger overwhelmingly, and effective September 1, 1986, we are now one college.

Organizationally, as might be expected, the promise of economies of scale has yet to be realized. (Cuff, 1986; Somervill, 1983) Rather, unanticipated merger expenses have arisen and there is a persistent tendency that must be checked regularly to want to remake the junior college campus over in the image of the other.

Considerable effort has also gone on to integrate the two cultures. The college president is available regularly on a weekly basis on the junior college campus as part of what Bastien (1986, p. 34) calls an "infiltration" effort. However, as might also be expected in a process so new, challenges remain. There are tendencies to refer in joint meetings to the "college," when all that is in fact being referenced is the major campus. In the junior college campus, also, responsibility for several functions might be combined in one person. Where tasks are collapsed in this way, it is often difficult to achieve consolidation with the acquiring college, where line responsibilities are more discreet.

In retrospect the experience would tend to support the observation that there is a considerable difference between knowing something and being able to affect the change as a result of that knowledge;colloquially, between knowing something and being able to do something about it! As an example, several studies point to the need for regular, reliable information to both organizations, particularly in the period of high anxiety. (Gall, 1986; Bastien, 1986; Iberman, 1985) Yet, because the notion of the merger had been discussed so openly and under immediate conditions at the junior college, it was much more a reality there-- as were its possible consequences and opportunities-- than was true at CSC. In addition, faculty at CSC resisted their consultation-only role in the merger discussions and expressed concern--and do even now-- that perhaps too much deference was being paid the "junior" partner--those who were referred to recently as "they--the plural inscrutable."

Despite these misgivings the merger has had positive short-term benefits already. The first is the obvious expansion of CSC's mission to include another educational market and location. According to a recently completed study conducted by the college's public relations firm, the merger has been perceived by the Twin Cities business community as a wise transaction. The challenge, revealed in the same study, is to have the action seen as shrewd business practice but to continue to market the campuses as quite distinct entities.

A second positive result of the merger is that it has triggered a reorganization of CSC operations, something that was widely discussed as needed years prior to the merger but implemented only now; legitimized perhaps by the intricate nature of newly combined operations.

A third positive result has been discussion surrounding joint academic programming. A faculty committee from both campuses is designing an approval process for the development of new joint programs. It has examined the program design process in place currently at both campuses and appears to be moving toward a recommendation that combines entrepreneurship on one hand with consensus-building on the other.

Another good result of the merger goes beyond what Thompson observed that "institutions of higher education historically have changed very slowly and in very small increments," and thus find mergers intolerable. (1985, p. 23) Rather, it is the realization that there is nothing immutable about our business, and that accommodation to opportunity is no vice.

Finally, though, there has been a gradual recognition not just of the complexities but of the possibilities of the new organization. If in the midst of the stress of what has been described by Marks and Mirvis as the "cascading of minor changes" post-merger (1985, p. 53), we can look beyond the immediate to the vision those possibilities nourish, we will prove ultimately, that we are able to do together what neither of us could do with such quality alone.

Bibliography

Ackerman, Linda S. "Transition Management: An In-depth Look at Managing Complex Change." Organizational Dynamics, 1982, pp. 46-66.

Barr, Robert D. "School of Education Mergers: Institutional Survival or Administrative Madness?" Journal of Teacher Education, July/August 1985, Vol. 36, 4, pp. 50-53.

Bastien, David T. "Common Patterns of Behavior and Communication in Mergers and Acquisitions." Unpublished paper. Minneapolis, Minnesota, University of Minnesota, 1985.

Blake, Robert R. and Jane Srygley Mouton. "How to Achieve Integration on the Human Side of the Merger." Solving Costly Organizational Conflicts: Achieving Intergroup Trust, Cooperation and Team Work. San Francisco: Jossey-Bass, Inc., 1984, pp. 41-56.

Cannon, Joan B. "The Organizational Human Implications of a Merger." Unpublished paper. American Educational Research Association, April 13, 1983.

Crossland, Fred E. "Learning to Cope with a Downward Slope," Change, July/August 1980, Vol. 12, 5, pp. 18, 22-25.

Cuff, Daniel. "Do Mergers Work?" New York Times, October 12, 1986, Section 12, pp. 5, 30.

Fadel, Virginia Ann and Nancy A. Carter. "Openings, Closings, Mergers and Accreditation Status of Independent Colleges and Universities: Winter 1970-Summer 1979." National Institute of Independent Colleges and Universities, June 1980.

Fisher, Ruth. "Case Western Reserve: Federation Fever," Change, October 1978, Vol. 10, pp. 38-43.

Gall, Adrienne L. (ed.) "Four by Four: What is the Role of HRD in a Merger?" Training and Development Journal, April 1986, pp. 18-23.

Greene, Janice S., Arthur Levine and Associates. _Opportunity in Adversity: How Colleges can Succeed in Hard Times_. San Francisco: Jossey-Bass, Inc., 1985.

Iberman, Arlyne J.   "The Human Elements of Mergers," _Management Review_, June 1985, pp. 35-7.

Konkel, Richard H. and Lewis D. Patterson.   "Sharing Collegiate Resources: The New Challenge: Guidelines to Facilitate Interinstitutional Sharing Based on a National Invitational Conference at Wingspread (Racine, Wisconsin, March 23-5, 1981), "Council for Interinstitutional Leadership, October 1981.

Marks, Mitchell Lee and Philip Mirvis, "Merger Syndrome: Stress and Uncertainty." _Mergers and Acquisitions_, Summer 1985, pp. 50-55.

Matlock, John and Frederick S. Humphries.   "The Planning of the   Merger of Two Public Higher Education Institutions: A Case Study of Tennessee State University and the University of Tennessee at Nashville," Paper presented at the Association of Institutional Research Annual Forum, San Diego, CA., May 13-17, 1979.

Mayhew, Lewis B.   _Surviving the Eighties_.   San Francisco: Jossey-Bass, Inc., 1979.

Millet, John D.   _Mergers in Higher Education: An Analysis of Ten Case Studies_. Washington D.C. : The American Council of Education, 1976.

Mingle, James R.   "Redirecting Higher Education in a Time of Budget Reduction: Issues in Higher Education," Southern Regional Education Board, 1982.

Morrisseau, James J.   "The Private Sector Revisited: NYU and P.I.N.Y.," _Planning for Higher Education_, December 1973, Vol. 2, <u>6</u>, pp. 7-10.

Nadler, David A.   "Managing Transitions to Uncertain Future States," _Organizational Dynamics_, Summer 1982, pp. 37-45.

"On Institutional Mergers and Acquisitions," _Academe_, April 1981, Vol. 66, <u>2</u>, pp. 83-5.

O'Neill, Joseph P. and Samuel Barnett. "Colleges and Corporate Change: Merger, Bankruptcy and Closure: A Source Book for Trustees and Administrators." Conference of Small Private Colleges, Princeton, New Jersey, March 1980.

Peters, Michael H. "Mergers of Institutions of Higher Education," College and University, Winter 1977, Vol. 52, 2, pp. 202-10.

Pritchett, Price. After the Merger: Managing the Shock Waves. Dallas, Pritchett & Associates, Inc., 1985

Shimeall, Kent. "Merger as a Remedy in Higher Education Desegregation." Univ of Toledo Law Review, 11, 3, Spring 1980, pp. 511-38.

Somervill, Christine Z. "Intra-institutional Mergers of Academic Units: Growth in the Context of Decline" ASHE 1983 Annual Meeting, March 1983.

Thompson, Hugh L. "Considering a Merger." Planning for Higher Education, Spring 1985, Vol.13, 3, p. 21-6.

DATE DUE

GAYLORD   PRINTED IN U.S.A